INTERNATIONAL
MARITIME FRAUD

INTERNATIONAL
MARITIME FRAUD

AUSTRALIA AND NEW ZEALAND
The Law Book Company Ltd.
Sydney : Melbourne : Perth

CANADA AND U.S.A.
The Carswell Company Ltd.
Agincourt, Ontario

INDIA
N.M. Tripathi Private Ltd.
Bombay
and
Eastern Law House Private Ltd.
Calcutta and Delhi
M.P.P. House
Bangalore

ISRAEL
Steimatzky's Agency Ltd.
Jerusalem : Tel Aviv : Haifa

MALAYSIA : SINGAPORE : BRUNEI
Malayan Law Journal (Pte.) Ltd.
Singapore and Kuala Lumpur

PAKISTAN
Pakistan Law House
Karachi

INTERNATIONAL MARITIME FRAUD

by

ERIC ELLEN,

Q.P.M., LL.B.(HONS.), C.B.I.M.

Director, International Maritime Bureau

and

DONALD CAMPBELL

of Gray's Inn, Barrister

LONDON
SWEET & MAXWELL
1981

Published in 1981 by
Sweet & Maxwell Limited of
11 New Fetter Lane, London
Printed in Great Britain by
Page Bros. (Norwich) Ltd.

Second Impression 1982
Third Impression 1983
Fourth Impression 1986

British Library Cataloguing in Publication Data

Ellen, Eric
    International maritime fraud
    1. Fraud   2. Shipping
    I. Title   II. Campbell, Donald
    364.1'63   HV6691

    ISBN 0–421–27150–7

Preface

Commercial fraud is a method of crime bringing to its practitioners rich rewards when successful and substantial punishments in failure. Within national boundaries, in spite of the inherent difficulties which stem from masses of documents and complexity of detail, fraud can be a relatively simple matter to investigate and prosecute. This only holds true if a particular deal or series of transactions is recognised to be fraudulent, when in almost every case, there will be material linking the offender to the crime. Thus, a reasonably competent investigator working within his own country and made aware of the crime, will often be able to identify those responsible and collect sufficient evidence to launch a prosecution. A truly successful fraud, by definition, is one that is either not seen to be fraud at all, or is committed by someone who cannot be linked to the machinery by which it was perpetrated.

In company with the United Kingdom, many nations have an organisation with the responsibility of investigating commercial crime and, whether they pass under the title of fraud squads, commercial branches or some similar off-shoot of a police force, their primary job is to investigate crimes which are substantially national in character.

This book is concerned with commercial fraud of a special kind, maritime fraud, which by its very nature is international. It is concerned with fraud in connection with the movement of goods from country to country across the great oceans; with dishonesty in the use of ships to transport those cargoes; with offences against those who fund the business interests involved, and with crimes against those who insure ships and cargoes. It sets out to describe typical frauds in order that they may, perhaps, be more readily recognised in future. It reviews the organisations and institutions whose job it is to facilitate international trade, as well as those who are concerned with the control of marine crime. It attempts to draw together many of the threads of world-wide criminal activity so that, with increased understanding, it may be better fought.

To achieve such objects in a form acceptable to a readership with widely different knowledge and experience, it is necessary to review, first the means by which international trade is financed, and then the laws which apply to such trade. This is not in any sense a technical manual for businessmen, lawyers, bankers or insurers so that each of them will find their own particular speciality covered in a simple manner. Each of them is asked, therefore, to be patient with the authors when these passages are reached and to bear in mind that other readers will profit from these relatively simple explanations.

If between these pages there is material which awakens public as well as commercial interests to the extent of maritime fraud, then one of its purposes will have been achieved. If it sparks off accelerated movement towards effective control of fraud, then that will be justification enough for a book on international maritime fraud.

Eric Ellen
Donald Campbell

London
1981

Contents

1 Introduction

For some 20 years or more frauds of a gigantic nature have been perpetrated throughout the world and many have had maritime connections.

As far as the United Kingdom is concerned, probably the most notorious fraudster of modern times was Emil Savundra who in 1959 was said to have master-minded the Costa Rican coffee fraud of over two million pounds. The frauds reported over the past few years are in the main carbon copies of the Costa Rican fraud but in reverse. The Costa Rican case involved goods—6,000 tons of coffee, one-tenth of that country's entire crop and their staple product—but no money was received to pay for it. In the present day deals there is money but no goods, just phantom shipments.

Savundra and his associates who bought the coffee were successful with their fraud because they convinced the Costa Rican financial advisers that due to currency regulations it was necessary to allow 180 days for payment. The amount of cash which Savundra received from this particular venture allowed him to go on to even greater frauds with his fire, auto and marine insurance operation for which he was subsequently convicted and sentenced to seven years imprisonment.

A fraud with maritime connections was one of the biggest in history and in 1965 its key figure was sentenced to 10 years imprisonment in a New Jersey court. This became known as "The Great Salad Oil Swindle" in which Anthony De Angelis borrowed vast sums of money on forged warehouse receipts for non-existent vegetable oil, which was purportedly being exported to under-developed countries under the United States "Food for Peace" programme of the 1950s and 1960s. The amount of money which is reported to have been obtained through the fraud was in the region of 200 million dollars. De Angelis went bankrupt in November, 1963 and almost caused another Wall Street crash. It is interesting to note that despite the De Angelis fraud few, if any, preventive measures were subsequently taken.

A Pulitzer prize winning author, Norman C. Miller, wrote:

"In Chicago, the Continental Illinois National Bank accepted receipts from Allied's (De Angelis' company) brokers, supposedly representing 331.5 million pounds of soybean oil worth over 30 million dollars. The bank thus accepted without question the dubious proposition that Allied was holding more than one third of the total soybean oil in the country, though the Census Bureau reports on food oil stocks showed it was impossible for Allied to have so much oil." (Extract from "The Great Salad Oil Swindle" by Norman C. Miller, published by Gollancz, p.146). Not only were the banks lax in this case but Miller said that very little has been done since De Angelis' exposure to correct the lax business conditions which made his swindle possible.

In latter years there has been a marked escalation of fraud in the maritime field and in 1979 there were an average of three frauds per month reported each of which represented a loss of approximately 1,000,000 U.S. dollars. Taking into account the fact that the greater number of charter party and documentary frauds are never aired in public, the 1979 figures can only represent the tip of the iceberg.

In those cases which were reported it was found that:

(a) The majority of the vessels involved were over 15 years of age.

(b) The majority of the vessels were on a single voyage charter.

An analysis of 93 cases reported up to November 1979 showed the following involvement of vessels by flags:

    Greece—46
    Panama—24
    Cyprus—16
    Spain—2
    Liberia, India, Singapore, South Korea, Sharjah—1 each

(Figures provided by the International Chamber of Commerce).

When considering these figures, however, it must be borne in mind that different countries have different shares of the world's merchant tonnage.

In the earlier days, the frauds were centred around Nigeria and the Arab countries of the Middle East. In these areas, ports were in the developmental stage and a rapid increase in imports caused ships to be delayed for weeks and even months whilst waiting for a discharge berth.

In some instances shipowners and charterers found themselves unable to wait because of economic and operational pressures and landed their cargo elsewhere. It did not take long for some to realise that this expedient, born of necessity could be turned to their own criminal advantage and they could sell the cargo. This they did, making use of those countries where the law on this type of activity was either defective or non-existent. As countries became aware of the problem and tightened their laws, the action shifted to other areas, notably the Lebanon.

Documentary type frauds came to light in the Far East and in this part of the world there was also a tremendous increase in ship sinkings. A leading marine investigator who was called upon to investigate numerous ship casualties involving cargo underwriters in millions of U.S. dollars, found that ships were being scuttled in the South China Seas where there was little opportunity to recover the cargoes or of discovering whether or not the cargo ever existed. Moreover, he found evidence of some ships being used to carry refugees from Vietnam, possibly after discharge of cargo into Vietnamese ports. He also discovered a correlation between the luxury goods in demand on the black market in Vietnam and the cargoes alleged to have been in the scuttled ships.

2 International Trade

As an opening to this study of international trade let us go back to prehistoric man. At his feet there is a lump of meat in which he, having gorged himself, has no further interest. His neighbour, perhaps unable to kill animals because of his weaker build, has learned to catch fish, collect berries and to identify the most edible leaves. Did the strong man choose not to see the weaker slowly pick up the meat, concentrating instead on savouring the interesting food put down in its place? Were they both so bored by the sameness of their diet that suspicion and jealousy encouraged an exchange of surpluses, and, was this the dawn of trade?

The next stage in a review of the birth of trade must be reached by a step of countless centuries, to a point where international trade was becoming established and here, one might consider the activities of a wine producer from, let us say, Brundisia. Having been fortunate in producing far more jars of wine than he could either use for himself or sell to his own countrymen, he may have had the idea of taking them by sea to sell on the quayside at Alexandria. He could then have decided to return via Carthage buying silks and ivory in the market with his profit from the wine, which in turn would find eager buyers at home at yet more profit.

Trade of such simplicity expanded to Europe and the British Isles from a time when the Phoenicians visited England in search of tin in exchange for which they bartered goods of approximately equal value. In due course gold and silver became symbols of value with the result that an exchange of goods between parties remote from each other became simpler and very much more flexible. From gold to national units of currency, exchange rates and the complexities of international accounting became an inevitable progression in a world where progress was tied to rapidly improving communications. An Omaha farmer with grain to sell could not load it into a ship in order to sell it around the Middle East ports, no more than could a Welsh mine owner attempt to sell his coal from a ship newly arrived in Stavanger. Thus it was that a system of international trading grew up based upon a merchantile law and custom which, with local adaption and variation, is accepted by traders throughout the world.

Principles

International trading can only take place within the bounds of an agreement between the parties and so varied are the dangers and difficulties facing those who engage in such trade, that a number of conventions have grown up to smooth their paths. For example, when does the seller relinquish ownership of his goods and the buyer take it over; who has the responsibility for insuring goods in transit; and who the right to claim when those goods are lost or damaged? Until one understands the broad principles governing overseas trading it is difficult to appreciate the elements which are affected where someone sets out to commit fraud.

International trading is based upon the simple contract of sale of goods. Smith in England wants to sell 100 steel girders to Khan in Pakistan and Khan wants to buy them. Ideally, Smith might like to load them on his own ship and convey them to Pakistan where Khan would unload them onto the quayside and give Smith the agreed price in cash. However commercial life is far too complicated for such a simple arrangement so that when striking their bargains, both parties must reach agreement on fundamental terms of which the most important is the price. Let us put a notional price upon Smith's girders of, say £1,000 "ex works." If Khan wants them at £1,000 then, having been quoted that price "ex works" he becomes the owner at the moment he or his agent collects them from Smith's foundry and conforms with the agreement as to payment. He might, instead, agree to buy them f.o.b. at, say, £1,025, and an agreement in such terms is much more likely than one stated to be "ex works" where the purchaser is based abroad without transport or warehousing facilities in the sellers country. Alternatively, the agreement might stipulate a price of, say, £1,200 on c.i.f. terms. These two groups of initials are no more than convenient cyphers describing the liabilities and obligations accepted by the contracting parties, but acquaintance with them is crucial to an understanding of marine fraud, for reasons which will become obvious in due course.

Explanation of Terms

F.o.b. stands for free on board and is instantly recognisable as delineating Smith's responsibilities:
1. (1) to deliver the girders, in good condition, to a port nominated in the contract by Khan and there to load them on to an effective ship;
2. (2) to pay all handling charges until the goods are loaded;

   (3) to complete all customs formalities;
   (4) to inform Khan in good time of the date of loading so that he can obtain insurance cover.

Khan's responsibilities are:
   (1) to inform Smith of the name and location of an effective ship to carry the girders, in sufficient time for Smith to get the goods alongside so that they may be loaded within the contract date;
   (2) to arrange adequate space aboard;
   (3) to pay freight on the cargo.

When Smith has carried out all his part of the contract, the girders will have been loaded in good condition on the proper ship in good time and Khan will have been given the opportunity to insure them on their journey. Smith will have been given a bill of lading by the ship's master, and will now look to Khan for payment in accordance with their prior arrangement.

In the case of a c.i.f. agreement their individual responsibilities will be quite different and, as will have been noticed, the price that Khan will pay will be greater. It should be made clear at this point that the notional figures given as an example bear no relation to reality, either as to cost price or to the cost of transport and insurance, but are given simply as an illustration of principles.

C.i.f. stands for cost, insurance and freight, or, the price of the girders together with the insurance premium and the carriage charges to the port of destination. In both c.i.f. and f.o.b. contracts, a port will be specified, one a port of departure and the other a port of arrival. In view of the different responsibilities of buyer and seller, these differences will be apparent. F.o.b. London means that the seller must deliver free on board, a pre-arranged ship at London docks, whilst c.i.f. Karachi means that his responsibility requires that he delivers on board a ship of his choice, at Karachi docks.

Smith in contracting to deliver c.i.f. Karachi, takes on the following responsibilities:
   (1) to load the girders in good condition on board ship within a stated period of time or, more likely, by an agreed date;
   (2) to pay freight charges from the port of departure until arrival at Karachi;
   (3) to obtain proper insurance for the value of the cargo from the time of shipment until delivery to the buyer;
   (4) to obtain a bill of lading, commercial invoice and any other specified documents and forward these together with assignable insurance documents to the buyer so that he may claim the goods from the ship.

An important factor to be noted when considering the differences between f.o.b. and c.i.f. contracts is that property, *i.e.* ownership, in the goods passes at different stages. In f.o.b. contracts, property passes from seller to buyer on shipment except where, somewhat unusually, this convention is not followed and the seller has reserved the right of disposal to himself. In c.i.f. contracts, however, property does not pass until payment has effectively been made by the buyer. Risk follows property so that the buyer in f.o.b. should, and the seller in c.i.f. must, insure the cargo throughout the sea voyage. The importance of understanding this is directly related to appreciating how some frauds are operated, particularly those aimed at insurance underwriters.

Another vital element of trade is the method of payment and we can dispose of f.o.b. contracts quite shortly. Generally, a buyer who makes an f.o.b. contract obtains ownership of the cargo upon loading and will have either paid the seller on loading or will have made a credit arrangement of one kind or another. It is logical to expect that when a seller has loaded his goods aboard the buyer's nominated vessel, he has lost control of them and will hardly do so without having first been paid. Payment in many c.i.f. contracts will be much more complicated and, once again, it is a subject with which the reader should be familiar. Before moving to the finance of international trade, however, the legal aspects should be introduced.

Introduction to Legal Principles

A c.i.f. contract is based upon the issue of a bill of lading by a carrier within the meaning of the Hague Rules. These rules, accepted by almost every nation as the basis for contracts of carriage, are an appendix to and form part of the Carriage of Goods by Sea Act 1971. A précis of these rules will be found in Appendix A to this book. Broadly speaking, the rules define what is meant by a carrier, a contract of carriage and other relevant matters. They define goods as anything other than live animals *and* goods stated in the bill of lading to be deck cargo, if so carried. They deal with the risks in sea carriage but, for the purposes of this outline of international trade, their most important function is to declare the responsibilities and liabilities of a carrier. The rules state that a carrier must exercise due diligence in making the carrying ship seaworthy, properly man, equip and supply it, and make it cargo-worthy. The difference between seaworthy and cargo-worthy should be emphasised. A seaworthy ship may be so strong and so well crewed that it can withstand any peril that might befall it. Such a ship may, however, be so constructed or maintained so inadequately that its holds cannot be kept completely dry in rough weather. No exporter of cereals, cement or other dry goods would agree that such a vessel was cargo-worthy.

The carrier must issue a bill of lading and at this stage the importance of this document will become obvious because it is evidence to show that the goods described therein have been loaded aboard. Not only does it act as the master's acknowledgement that he has taken the goods aboard his ship, but it is also the shipper's guarantee of accuracy in describing their nature and quantity. Returning for a moment to the hypothetical contract between Smith and Khan, we now know it to be a c.i.f. agreement and in accordance with the Hague Rules, the master of the *SS. Wanderer* will have loaded the girders into his ship's hold and then issued Smith with a bill of lading. A bill of lading has another quality which has not yet been considered and that is that it can be transferred from party to party maintaining its function as a valid legal document with each transfer.

We know that Smith is obliged to insure the girders but not just any insurance policy will do, for this too must have certain qualities of which transferability is vital. The insurance, arranged by the issue of an underwriter's "slip," backed by a more formal policy, must conform to certain conventions which can be summarised as follows:

(1) The benefit of the insurance must be freely transferable from party to party.
(2) It must have been taken out with a reputable company and be drawn to a proper commercial standard.
(3) It must cover the full c.i.f. cost of the contract.

Transferability is an obvious quality in this kind of trading because when ownership of the goods passes from seller to buyer, it follows that insurance cover must move from one party to another. The remaining requirements are logical ones which need concern us no further for the purposes of this particular study.

Smith must also provide a proper commercial invoice which adequately describes the goods with proper marks as an aid to identification, and in addition, any other documents which must be produced at the port of arrival before the goods will be released. This group of documents, bill of lading, insurance and invoice become the instrument by which risk and ownership of goods passes from seller to buyer and by which the seller is paid. Smith is quite clearly not going to travel with his girders in order to deliver them in exchange for cash, nor one may assume, does he have a trusted agent in Karachi, who will make the exchange for him. It is through the world's banking system therefore that Smith will get his money, by means of a system of documentary credits.

Financial Provisions

The Smith-Khan transaction will be paid for by means of a bill of exchange, a document defined by section 3(1) of the Bills of Exchange

Act 1882 as " . . . an unconditional order in writing, addressed by one person to another, signed by the person giving it, requiring the person to whom it is addressed to pay on demand or at some fixed or determinable future time a sum certain in money to or to the order of a specified person, or to bearer." The contract between Smith and Khan was made on the agreement that payment would be by a bill of exchange and would conform to the Uniform Rules for the Collection of Commercial Paper, 1967. These rules are published by the International Chamber of Commerce in order to simplify trade and to minimise expensive disputes over the precise terms of contracts.

The transfer of goods for money begins when Smith draws a bill, addressed to Khan, requiring Khan to pay £1,200 within 90 days of sight, and lodges this bill with his bankers. With the bill he also hands over the shipping documents, namely the bill of lading, insurance and invoice. On receipt of these, the bank will discount the bill of exchange that is to say will pay Smith its face value, less an agreed percentage. Thus he has disposed of his goods and been paid for them at a slightly lower price than if it had been a straightforward cash sale. No doubt, however, he will have taken into account the shortfall in quoting a c.i.f. price to Khan.

Smith has his money, the bank has all those documents necessary for them to retain effective control of the goods until payment, the master of the *SS. Wanderer* has physical control of 100 steel girders, whilst Khan has an insurable interest. At this stage Khan comes into the picture because it is to his bank that the documents will eventually be transmitted, to allow him to collect the girders. Before he can do so, however, Smith's bank must be sure that the bill of exchange will be honoured and they will send it, by air, to Khan's bank. They being satisfied with him as a credit-worthy customer to whom they can look with confidence for payment, will agree to act with Smith's bank in the transaction upon which Smith's bank will send them the shipping documents.

At this stage in the transaction, Smith's bank has paid Smith and has lost control of the shipping documents and, of course, control of the legal right by lien to the goods represented by them. They will have received in return either payment by Khan's bank or a guarantee of payment. Khan's bank now has control of the documents of title and an arrangement whereby Khan will reimburse it for the price.

Let us move forward to the time when the *SS. Wanderer* is nearing Karachi and Khan wishes to make arrangements for collection of the girders. Before the master will relinquish physical control over the girders, he will require evidence that they are going to the right person and, for his purposes this will be whoever has possession of the shipping documents. Before Khan's bank will give up the shipping documents, it will have to be satisfied that payment is going to be made, or is being made at the time. In this instance they simply require acceptance by Khan of Smith's bill of exchange and, having his signature upon it as acceptor, release the shipping documents to him. Khan then collects his girders from the *SS. Wanderer* and the transaction is complete.

Figure 1

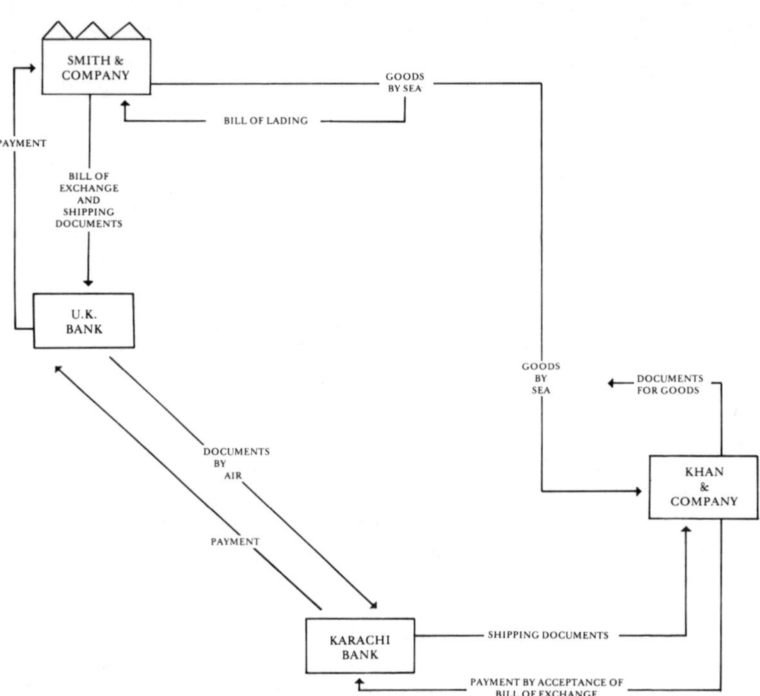

In order to make a relatively difficult transaction easier to follow, figure 1 sets it out in diagrammatic form. The reader to whom the subject of financing international trade is something new should be aware that Smith's deal with Khan is not by any means the most complicated. Whole books have been written on bills of exchange, bills of lading, documentary credits and many other elements of the subject. There could easily be more banks concerned than just two. There could be more than one buyer and shipping documents so drawn as to permit delivery of part cargo to each. There might easily be more than one seller having an interest in the price and very complicated credit arrangements could be written into the contract of sale.

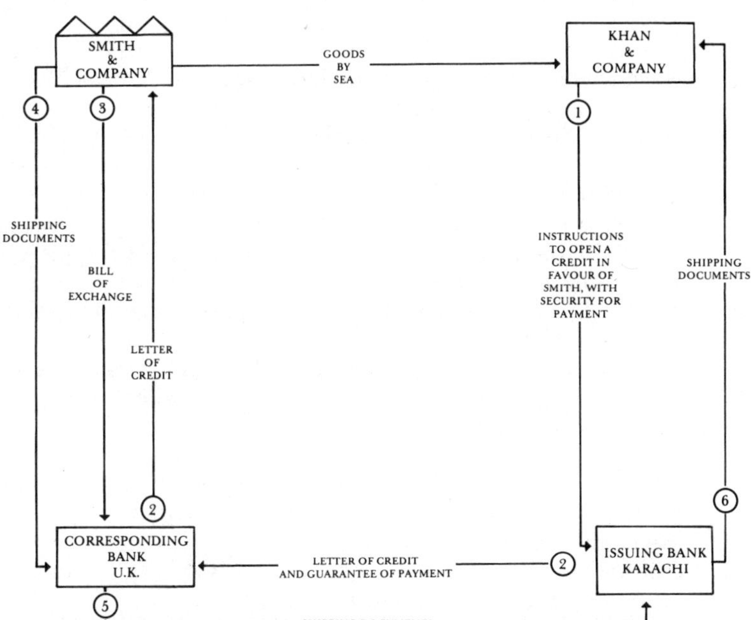

Figure 2 shows in diagrammatic form a transaction in which payment is made by the use of a documentary credit and, as will be seen later, these documentary credits are frequently at the core of a large number of frauds. The contract of sale is on c.i.f. terms, the buyer, Khan, agreeing to set up a credit arrangement under which Smith will be paid by the United Kingdom bank upon tender of agreed shipping documents. Those documents will be the bill of lading, insurance policy, commercial invoice and a certificate of dimension and quality issued by Steel Inspection (U.K.) Ltd. Before reaching that stage, however, the position should be reviewed. The goods are now aboard the *SS. Wanderer* en route for Karachi and Smith has his shipping documents all in order. Thus he has a receipt for them in the form of a bill of lading, an insurance document giving cover for the price including expenses of travel, and the other documents which form part of the necessary group. Now let us look at figure 2 in more detail to remind ourselves of the chain of events.

(1) Khan sets up his line of credit by giving his bankers the necessary instructions and security for the price. He will tell his bank what documents, in addition to the universally accepted ones, must be tendered before the price is paid over

to the seller. Khan's bank can now be referred to as the "issuing bank" because in due course it will issue a "letter of credit."

(2) The issuing bank sends the letter of credit to the U.K. bank. Such terms as Smith and Khan have agreed will be detailed in this letter of credit so that when Smith tenders shipping documents to the United Kingdom bank, the banker will be able to confirm their adequacy. The letter of credit is sent by the United Kingdom bank to Smith. The situation as between the parties is now that the issuing bank has security for the price and therefore guarantees the payment to the United Kingdom bank. The United Kingdom bank will pay over the price to Smith as soon as he has completed his part of the transaction, *i.e.* tendered the proper set of documents.

(3) Smith issues a bill of exchange to his bank, from now on called the corresponding bank. (Sometimes called the accepting or paying bank).

(4) Smith loads the steel aboard the *SS. Wanderer*, receiving in return, the bill of lading. Together with the other documents he tenders this to the corresponding bank and receives his payment in the form described.

(5) The corresponding bank exchanges the shipping documents with the issuing bank in return for the price.

(6) The issuing bank exchanges the shipping documents with Khan in return for the price.

(7) Khan collects his steel from the *SS. Wanderer* and the transaction is complete.

From the above it will be seen that there are two quite distinct elements to this particular transaction, typical of the vast majority of international sales. First there is the sale of goods, the provision of documents covering ownership, description and indemnity as the first element, then the transfer for value of the documents from party to party as the second. Smith and Khan are primarily interested in steel girders and the price: the banks are interested only in documents and security for the price. This is well illustrated in the words of section 8 of the "Uniform Customs and Practice for Documentary Credits" (1974) revision, issued by the International Chamber of Commerce:

> "In documentary credit operations, all parties concerned deal in documents and not in goods."

Smith and Khan are honest men who have concluded a transaction similar to countless others that are completed worldwide each year without difficulty. That the transaction was so happily achieved was because each of the documents concerned was genuine. Steel Inspections (U.K.) Ltd., respected by both parties, provided a satisfactory certificate of dimension and quality; the *SS. Wanderer's* master issued a clean bill of lading, an insurance of proper commercial standard was effected, and an adequate invoice was prepared. But what if one or more of those documents had not been authentic? What if Smith had been a dishonest man whose business interests were more widespread than simply to manufacture and sell steel girders? Where examples of international marine frauds are illustrated, the significance of these questions will be seen, as will the role of dishonest shipmasters, charterers and others.

Appendix B illustrates a typical group of shipping documents such as are used in hundreds of transactions each day throughout the world.

3 Ship Ownership

Closely bound up with the carriage of goods by sea is the question of control of ships by which those goods are carried. Control, in this context, is that exercised by whoever has the right to determine freight rates, acceptable classes of cargo and routes. Control of these factors may stem from more than a single base, the most obvious being a right to do so arising from simple ownership of the vessel.

There are thousands of merchant ships plying their trade all over the world. A very large proportion can be excluded from consideration in a study of maritime dishonesty, first of these being ships of the Eastern Bloc countries whose fleets are in government ownership as is their machinery for exporting goods. Next, one can take away fleets whose sole function is to move their own company's produce. Examples of these can be found in particular, in the oil and meat industries where a conglomerate owns the oil wells and ranches, shipping companies for transport, and finally retail outlets for their commodity. Of the large number remaining, further classifications must be made into those in corporate ownership and those in private hands: those forming part of a fleet and those in single vessel ownership; some on regular "liner" routes and others that "tramp" from port to port wherever their cargo takes them. Any of these can attract the fraudsman. Sometimes the fraud has no other connection with the ship other than as the source of a bill of lading and a means of transport, sometimes the ship itself is at the core when its loss provides the profit. This kind of crime can be committed against a vessel's operators, or by its operators against insurance companies, buyers of goods or less usually, against the shippers.

Charterparties

An owner's control of shipping is often relinquished for a time when his ship is hired to someone else under a charterparty, a document providing evidence of the contract between an owner and another, the charterer, for that hiring. There are three forms in which a charter may be arranged.

(1) *Voyage charter*

In this case a shipper may hire a ship to carry his goods between pre-determined ports, using either the total capacity for his own cargo or filling only a part with his and carrying other people's goods in the remaining space. In some instances the hirer may not have goods of his own, but will engage in a voyage charter agreement as a speculation by arranging carriage of other people's goods.

(2) *Time charter*

With this form of charter a vessel is hired for a period to trade anywhere and in any kind of cargo providing there are no specific restrictions against them contained in the charterparty.

(3) *Charter by demise/Bareboat charter*

This form of charter is the least usual and involves the charterer taking over the ship in its entirety for a period, becoming responsible for supplying crew, provisions and bunkering.

Voyage Charters

The problem of fitting ships to cargoes and cargoes to ships with a degree of efficiency is a complex business. The average manufacturer wishing to sell abroad but with no ship of his own, must find space in a suitable ship destined for his customer's country, sailing within the time appointed by the contract of sale. This is clearly a difficult matter, not usually a welcome task to one without extensive contacts in the shipping world, and therefore a market has developed over hundreds of years in which specialists act as intermediaries between shippers and ship owners in order to match ships with cargoes. The Baltic Exchange, commonly accepted name for the Baltic Mercantile and Shipping Exchange, situated in London, is the world's largest freight market dealing with many aspects of cargo movement by air and sea. A seller wishing to ship goods c.i.f. and having no ships of his own will require space in a suitable *general ship*, that is to say a ship carrying cargo for reward on behalf of more than one shipper. He will obtain the services of a *chartering agent* whose function is that of a broker finding available cargo space. He, in turn, will negotiate with a *shipbroker* who acts for shipowners in providing cargo space so that between them the shipper's requirements will be met. In addition to these, there are *independent brokers* who will act for either shipper or shipowner. There is no statutory requirement that obliges either party to a contract of carriage to employ brokers operating within the Baltic Exchange and many agreements are made outside the market.

The words of Mr. Gordon Hutton of Lloyds Marine Market, addressing a conference of international insurers, point out the

current situation, and the possible dangers of trading outside an
accepted market:

"We are naive if we imagine that most chartering is still done in the
traditional manner, on the Baltic Exchange in London or in the
Tanker Market in New York—it is more likely now to be on the
quayside, office to office, or in some backyard, where 'fly-by-night'
operators set up temporary quarters. This makes it all the easier to
by-pass respectability."

Time Charters

Time charterers may within the terms of the charterparty reserve to
themselves the right to issue bills of lading which, as has been
discussed earlier, act as receipts and documents of title. In sound
commercial practice a charterer will issue bills which conform to the
description of cargo loaded aboard by confirming weight, description and apparent good order with the mate's receipts. Since a
master's bills of lading are drawn up from mate's receipts, it is quite
reasonable to assume that they will be proper documents for
charterers to use for that purpose. The charterer knowing from those
receipts what has been loaded aboard, issues the bills of lading which
then becomes evidence of such loading and upon tender by a buyer,
the document of title. If the charterer has no intention of observing
the time honoured commercial customs, and intends to defraud the
purchasers and perhaps put the shipowner in jeopardy as well, there
is no reason why, having obtained the mate's receipts, he should not
draw up a dishonest bill of lading and, providing it is tendered
properly with all other required documents, obtain his money. On
arrival at the port of destination buyer and master are then left to
reconcile a bill of lading giving title to 1,500 tons of steel supposedly
in a ship physically incapable of holding more than 1,000 tons.

The law relating to those maritime operations within the scope of
this book can be conveniently if somewhat simplistically divided into
two: civil law dealing with disputes between the contracting parties in
charters, insurances and contracts of carriage; and criminal law to
accommodate crimes of a wide variety.

Civil Remedies

The civil law in its mercantile application, developed since the Middle
Ages and international in flavour, is complicated but nevertheless
effective in settling disputes between merchant and merchant. These
disputes must be resolved in the courts of a country agreed between

the parties in dispute or, when they cannot settle the proper venue between themselves, in such a court as is decided for them. When parties contract, they will sometimes agree that the "proper law of contract" shall be that of a particular country, thus removing one area of difficulty if a dispute arises. However, many agreements are made without stipulating the "proper law" to be applied and the parties must then either agree or seek a court ruling as to where the action ought to be tried.

Typical of the problems which can arise, and which the courts are quite capable of resolving is that of *Rossano* v. *Manufacturers' Life Insurance Ltd.* [1963] 2 Q.B. 352. This was a decision in a dispute over an insurance contract. It had nothing to do with ships or shipping but is an excellent example of a court's ability to sift international problems into their proper categories and to pronounce a result with authority.

The plaintiff, P, was an Egyptian who in 1940 entered into three endowment insurance agreements with the insurance company, D, whose head office was in Ontario, Canada, but whose branches were established in many countries throughout the world. The contracts, effected through the insurer's Cairo office were written in English and provided for two of the policies, on maturity, to be paid in sterling by banker's demand drafts drawn on London. The third policy was to be paid in dollars by banker's demand drafts on New York.

In the years between contract and maturity, the Egyptian authorities obtained garnishee orders on D's Cairo branch in respect of taxes due to the government from P. The effect of these orders was that when the insurance money became due, D would be obliged to pay it, not to P but to the Egyptian authorities. D faced a further problem in that exchange control regulations forbade the transfer of funds out of Egypt without government consent which, in the light of the garnishee orders was unlikely to be given. D therefore refused to pay the money and claimed that:

(a) As the proper law of contract was Egyptian because the contract was to be performed in Egypt, payment elsewhere to an Egyptian national without government consent would be illegal, and

(b) as there were two garnishee orders restraining the company from paying P in Egypt, payment to P there would result in a penalty by the authorities for breach of the orders and, perhaps, the risk of having to pay the money twice.

Mr. Justice McNair gave judgment for the plaintiff on the grounds that the proper law of contract was that of the Province of Ontario because:

(a) The policy form of which there were various kinds, was one based upon the law of Ontario.

(b) The terms had to be accepted by executives of the company in Ontario.

(c) No alteration of terms or assignments would be made without authority from home based executives.

(d) Payment was to be made against surrender of the policies to the Ontario office.

It followed from his judgement that D must pay P by the contracted method, by bankers demand draft on London, in pounds sterling.

There are, of course, numerous cases of a similar nature where tangled international situations have responded to judicial unravelling, but perhaps Rossano will suffice as a simple and convincing example.

Criminal Actions

What has been said about the ability of the civil law to solve disputes does not help innocent parties where a contract of carriage, insurance or other purpose is affected by crime. A transaction that has gone wrong through criminal action may involve several innocent parties, each having claims against the other and although a court may resolve differences between them, there are going to be two parties remaining outside that settlement. One will be the criminal who has gained from the original crime, the other will be the innocent party upon whom the loss eventually falls. At this stage the criminal law is, or should be, available to deal with the criminal. Unfortunately, the criminal law when looked at from an international aspect, is so uncoordinated that action against criminals whose activities are not confined to a single country becomes at the very least difficult and all too often impossible. The concept of theft is universal but even the sanctions against it vary from the radical punishment of Islam, amputation of a hand, through imprisonment for varying periods, to penalties such as fines, probation and restitution. Piracy, too, may be universally proscribed with severe penalties but beyond these relatively simple concepts, nations have very different attitudes, criteria and laws.

Take a simple example. A Nigerian agrees to buy a number of sewing machines from an English dealer c.i.f. Lagos and makes a documentary credit arrangement. The goods are loaded aboard a Panamanian registered vessel, whose Greek master issues a clean bill of lading. The seller, having properly insured the cargo and prepared a commercial invoice, tenders the agreed shipping documents to the appropriate bank and is paid for his goods. Unknown to the seller, the vessel's master is also its owner and that particular name is just one in a succession of others under which it has sailed in recent months. In a sudden storm, unrecorded by the world's weather reporting service, the ship and her entire cargo slips beneath the waves into water of such depth that she is never likely to be seen again. Her crew are all saved. The Nigerian buyer, along with perhaps a dozen others whose cargo was lost, must now claim on the insurance, suffering delay in his business plans and a good deal of delay in securing payment.

But what if the ship has not vanished beneath the waves but becomes submerged, once again, in a new identity and her cargo sold off in some Middle East port? Let us assume that some astute observer has spotted the ship discharging the "lost" cargo in Beirut and through the agency of a member of the International Association of Airport and Seaport Police has informed their coordination centre in London. The uninitiated will, at this point, expect the law to step in and take action against the dishonest master and crew. The initiated will regret once more that the law is virtually impotent unless good fortune delivers the offender into its hands. In this simple example, by United Kingdom law, the master has committed a theft of the property at the very least, certainly a conspiracy to cheat and defraud the insurers, and has probably obtained freight by deception. Had he landed in England following his alleged sinking, and sufficient evidence been available, he would have been liable to conviction of some or all of those offences in a United Kingdom criminal court. No doubt, too, had he landed in Nigeria, he would have been subject to the sanctions provided by Nigerian criminal law. Can Lebanese law, for example, cope with the criminal aspects of such a case? Would the Lebanese wish to prosecute the master if they could? What about the Greek authorities whose compatriot the master is? With no firmer connection than that, they are unlikely to launch a prosecution even if their system of law provides a suitable power. In the case of Panama, the ship's flag is one of convenience and the ship owes Panama no more than its registration fee and compliance with minimal requirements. Nor does Panama interfere in the running of its cosmopolitan fleet by undertaking to discipline such offending masters. No court, regrettably, would rule upon the question of venue for trial except as a rhetorical question because, were it to order the master to appeal before it to determine venue, there exists little power to enforce the order against one who is out of the jurisdiction.

If, however, the legal authorities of one country decide that they have sufficient evidence to prove an offence known to their law against someone who is out of the jurisdiction, they must consider extradition if they wish to pursue the matter.

The transfer of fugitive offenders between Commonwealth

countries is covered by the provisions of the Fugitive Offenders Act 1967 but in this hypothetical case one would have to turn to the Extradition Act 1870 and subsequent amending statutes. The first question is whether or not an extradition treaty exists between the United Kingdom and whichever country it is known an offender has gone. Treaties are made with individual nations and the terms of each treaty will cater for the particular needs expressed between them. A very common term of any treaty is that each nation reserves the right not to surrender its own nationals to the applying power. In the United Kingdom only the Home Secretary has discretion to waive that right, a waiver that is not lightly exercised because, in common with most nations, there is a repugnance against such a course. One essential term of each treaty is that its catalogue of extraditable offences will not include offences which are not common to both powers in essential features. Theft of goods of value would, quite clearly, be common to any nations negotiating a treaty however the crime might be described. Other matters may not be so clear cut—in some countries it is a criminal offence to issue a cheque upon an account in which there are no funds, in the United Kingdom it is not *necessarily* so. All treaties are made on the basis that its parties will not extradite for political crimes. In recent years there have been enormous difficulties in relationships between the United Kingdom and the Republic of Ireland whose Extradition Act 1965, whilst permitting extradition in principle, hedges it about with so many obstacles that it is almost a dead letter. Irish law does not permit extradition where the crime alleged is "connected with a political offence." An armed robbery has been held to be connected with a political offence providing its perpetrators can claim to have been collecting funds for a political group; that the group is an illegal one proscribed by Irish law does not make any difference.

It is perhaps of interest to cite a real example: how a simple fraud prosecution can be frustrated by such a liberal interpretation of the law. A fraudsman with bogus qualifications including a doctorate of Homoeopathy and a degree in mechanical engineering, began operations as a finance broker. In this venture he collected money from people hoping to buy modest homes, as advance fees for the mortgages he was supposedly arranging. Having collected a great deal of this "front end" money without ever arranging a single effective mortgage, he de-camped to Dublin where he set up his plate as a homoeopath. His arrival was followed by a bank staff's strike which closed all Irish banks for about six months. As there could be no lodgements of credits or collection on cheques, cash circulated throughout the country against these documents awaiting a day when the banks could re-open. The doctor of course joined the fun and for half a year issued cheques which had no backing at his bank. Application was made to the Irish authorities under the Backing of Warrants (Republic of Ireland) Act 1965 for his surrender and in due course the offender appeared before the President of the Irish High Court. He claimed immunity on the basis that he was wanted in England, not for offences of fraud, but because he had been a source of finance and information to Irish extremists in that country. At great trouble and expense these counter allegations were proved to be utter non-sense and accepted to be so by the Irish courts. Nevertheless, by a series of delaying tactics, matters could not be resolved and when the Irish authorities asked, some three years after the initial application, whether or not the English police wished to make a fresh application, they were told in diplomatic terms that they were welcome to keep the offender and deal with him as they thought fit.

Not every application will meet with difficulties of such a character but one must nevertheless recognise that extradition, as a means of bringing a travelling criminal to trial, is likely to be time consuming and with only a marginal chance of success. Occasionally a state will declare an alien *persona non-grata* and, regardless of what efforts are in hand to extradite him, will simply expel him by placing him aboard a ship or aircraft whose destination is that country where his presence is eagerly sought. Against that one sees that even where all other circumstances favour rendition of a suspect, either under an extradition treaty or as a commonwealth fugitive offender, there remains a political discretion in the Home Secretary by which he can refuse.

If there is a lesson to be learned from this brief review of the means by which offenders may be brought before a court, it is that prevention is infinitely better than cure and whilst crime can never be cured, remedy can be almost impossible to achieve, faced with the difficulties of extradition.

Geneva Convention on the Territorial Sea and the Contiguous Zone 1958

At various places in this book there will be seen reference to the difficulties in attempting to legislate internationally in a truly effective way, whether for purely commercial purposes or for the control and punishment of crime. The stumbling block is always essentially that of sovereignty which is strongly maintained in regard to the law of the sea. Central to any discussion on this subject is the Geneva Convention on the Territorial Sea and the Contiguous Zone 1958, together with an outline sketch of the *Corfu Channel* case.

In 1946, a group of British warships sailed through the Corfu Channel which had been swept clear of mines but were fired upon by Albanian gunners. Later, a larger force of British warships again passed through the channel but two of their number struck sea mines, suffering severe damage and loss of life. Later still, Royal Navy minesweepers cleared the channel of mines, discovered that those destroyed were of German manufacture, and concluded that they had been newly laid after the initial sweeping operation. The matter came before the International Court of Justice on three separate occasions and judgments were entered:

25th March 1948. The Court found that it had jurisdiction despite Albania's contention that it had not.

9th April 1949. The Court found that Albania was responsible for the explosions, taking the view that although it had not been proved that the Albanian government actually ordered the mines to be laid, they must have known of it. Albania counterclaimed that Britain had violated Albanian sovereignty by sending warships through its territorial waters, and by minesweeping in the aftermath of the explosions. In regard to the counterclaim, the Court found that the British ships were engaged in innocent passage and did not therefore violate Albania's sovereignty, but by carrying out a minesweeping operation had done so.

December 15 1949. The Court assessed reparations due from the Albanian government at over three-quarters of a million pounds in respect of damage to the ships and injury and loss of life.

The *Corfu Channel* case formed a basis for discussion and the Court's judgment can be seen reflected in the Geneva Convention, particularly in Articles 14. 15. 16. 17. and 23., which deal with innocent passage in respect of merchant, government and war-ships.

Much of the Convention is of interest only to those whose concern is with fishing rights or pollution, both emotive and highly sensitive topics at the present time, but Article 19. deals with limitations on criminal jurisdiction and Article 20. with civil. So important is the Convention to those interested in maritime fraud and crime generally, that the text is reproduced at Appendix C for a more careful study. Article 19. is particularly worthy of special consideration because it seems to give some authority for dealing with ships passing through territorial waters, upon which there has been some crime committed. Paragraph 5. of Article 19. imposes a limitation likely to prove fatal to the article's effectiveness, in that it inhibits coastal states from taking steps to arrest any person, or to conduct an investigation in connection with any crime committed before the ship entered territorial waters. Thus it would have been impossible, within the law, to have arrested the crew of the *Salem* (see chapter 5) whilst aboard a rescue vessel passing through a state's territorial waters even though that state might have been a victim of any crime committed.

The onus for arresting an offender who has committed an offence in international waters, or to make an investigation aboard the ship, rests firmly upon the authorities of the flag state, a patchy and generally uncertain remedy for those who have suffered loss or injury.

International law is based upon customs which are accepted by the majority of states, or by more formal agreements between them. Article 38(1) of the Statute of the International Court of Justice (see Appendix D) sets out the law that it shall apply to any disputes submitted to it. International conventions, international customs as evidence of a generally accepted law, the general principles of law accepted among civilised nations and the teachings of eminent jurists are the cement which bind international law together and although they are less than effective in dealing with maritime crime, it should be said that they cope adequately with civil disputes. Shaw, in his book *International Law*, puts the matter neatly into perspective:

> "Contrary to popular belief, states do observe international law and violations are comparatively rare. The trouble is, however, that such violations (like armed attacks and racial oppression) are well publicised and strike at the heart of the system, the creation and preservation of international peace and justice. But just as incidents of murder, robbery and rape do occur within national legal orders without bringing down the whole edifice or stimulating citizens to deny that law exists, so, analogously, assaults upon international legal rules point to the weaknesses of the system without denigrating their validity or their necessity.
>
> However, apart from the occasional gross violation the vast majority of the provisions of international law are followed."

While discussing sovereignty in relation to the international system of justice, mention should be made of the Court of Justice of the European Communities, if only to show that it is more or less powerless in matters of maritime crime. The Court has 10 judges at the present time, one from each of the member states, and deals with disputes between those states as well as interpreting Community laws. As with the International Court of Justice, it acts only with the consent of the member states, such consent being given by virtue of having adopted the Treaty of Rome. No case involving international maritime fraud has been brought before it at the time of writing.

4 Classification of Maritime Crimes

In making a study of possible methods of classifying maritime frauds, one can select any one of a number of possible divisions, each of which has some attraction. In the F.E.R.I.T.[1] report, crimes are classified into hull frauds and cargo frauds. Such a simple division has only limited appeal, because many frauds are aimed at both hull and cargo. A further classification could be by victim, but again there are obvious difficulties where there is a multiplicity of victims in one single fraud, a situation which applies to a very large percentage. Although the immediate victim may be a ship owner or the consignee of cargo, in most cases there will be insurers in the background who, in due time, have to take a large proportion of any losses.

The method decided upon for the purposes of this book, is to use a broad classification into four types of crime. The reader will be aware by now, however, that a measure of overlap must necessarily exist between these broad groups in many cases, and, in fact, there are many occasions when an element of each is bound to exist in a single crime. The broad classifications are:

  (a) Documentary frauds.
  (b) Frauds in connection with charters.
  (c) Scuttling.
  (d) Cargo thefts.

As an introduction to actual cases in which these kinds of crime are well illustrated, there follows an outline of the ways in which the four might well arise.

Documentary fraud

The scale and variety of frauds in connection with shipping documents is vast and of those documents, the bill of lading is the most likely vehicle, although by no means the only one. Letters of credit, certificates of quality, certificates of origin and invoices may all have a part to play in the successful perpetration of a maritime fraud. The reason why a great number of such frauds have been committed lies in the quality possessed by the bill of lading and associated papers making up a set of shipping documents. Except where a bill is not

[1] Far East Regional Investigation Team Report 1979, commissioned by the insurance markets of the Region with the support of the London market

endorsed, as for example where a family ships their own goods overseas to the country to which they are emigrating, or where shipper and consignee are merely parts of the same business group, the bill will be negotiable. One can appreciate that goods shipped under a bill of lading will have a more than nominal value, so that possession of an endorsed bill gives the holder eventual physical control of those goods or the value they represent. Remembering this, let us look again at the Smith/Khan transaction, but this time with one of the parties being dishonest. Let us also change the commodity in question, to a consignment of valuable chemicals, packed into drums upon each of which the chemical's name is stencilled, together with other leading marks. Which of the two is more likely to try to defraud the other?

Khan, as purchaser in Pakistan, can have no control over the shipment and must rely upon receiving shipping documents which agree with the goods he has ordered. For the purposes of this illustration, Khan receives from his bank a "clean" bill of lading, that is to say a bill upon which the master acknowledges receipt aboard of 1,000 drums, in apparent good order and condition, said to contain the chemical XYZ. Together with the bill there is an invoice giving details of the commodity and a certificate of quality issued by a chemist. Both of these documents show details sufficient for Khan to satisfy himself that the goods he will eventually receive will be those that he ordered. Khan's opportunity for fraud is somewhat limited. To forge his copy of the bill raising the number of barrels from 1,000 to 1,500 would be a possible means of attempting to defraud the insurance company. Such naive behaviour would be doomed to failure simply because the most elementary enquiries would reveal that copies of the bill and other documents did not agree with that presented to the master by Khan. It would be a foolish master who released cargo to a man holding a bill so vastly different from the actual quantity aboard, or on the authority of a bill which did not correspond with the ship's manifest. Khan can be ruled out of any question of fraud upon the bill of lading.

He cannot be excluded, however, from the possibility of criminal motives in connection with quality. With steel girders whose number and apparent condition are obvious, fraud might be rather difficult to accomplish. This is not so, however, when the goods are not of a kind susceptible to full inspection at the time of loading aboard a ship. The master does not have facilities for sampling the contents of drums and must accept them aboard on a "said to contain" basis, relying for his information upon details supplied by Smith and, perhaps the stencilled description upon each drum. Having obtained delivery of the cargo, Khan might conceivably substitute water for chemicals and then make a claim upon the insurers whose certificate forms part of the shipping documents. Such a fraud might well work, crude as it is, because any enquiry would have to resolve the question of which party was dishonest, with insurers being obliged to pay up and recover damages from the criminal. Khan, then would seem to be an unlikely prospect when searching for the dishonest party in a documentary fraud.

Much more likely is the proposition that Smith could be dishonest. He has control of the transaction from start to finish, by virtue of having control of the preparation and obtaining of both goods and shipping documents. He might, for example, fill the drums with material not of the quality demanded knowing that there is no possibility of his deception being discovered for several weeks. The drums may contain chemicals of a much inferior quality than that ordered, even perhaps water having no value at all. When once he has his bill of lading, tender to the United Kingdom bank of that and other necessary documents will result in his being paid, safe in the knowledge that his fraud will not come to light for a sufficient time during which he may well vanish. That would not, of course, be a true documentary fraud unless it were necessary to have supplied a false certificate of quality. For such a transaction to have taken place between Smith and Khan, a certificate would almost certainly have been stipulated in the letter of credit.

Smith might decide to commit his crime by means of documents forged after shipment. In such a situation, he will load a lesser quantity of drums than agreed with Khan, but tender documents showing that he has supplied the full quantity. Once again there will inevitably be considerable delay before Khan discovers the fraud when, on trying to collect his full consignment, the lesser number of drums is aboard. Forgery of this kind may range from the crude to the highly sophisticated. Simple alteration of a bill, with suitable adjustments to other shipping documents may well be sufficient to pass muster if Smith is discounting the documents through a speculator. They may well be detected however, if tendered to a vigilant banker, particularly when the corresponding bank is in possession of a copy bill. The situation is quite different however when Smith is not only shipper but also charters the ship upon which Khan's goods are loaded, because then he is entitled to issue bills in his own right. Examples of this will be seen in the illustrating cases later in this book, even to the extent where bills were issued for a cargo of weight far in excess of what the ship in which it was supposed to be loaded was capable of carrying.

Certificates of quality are documents issued by what should be independent inspectors who certify that the goods conform to whatever criteria is appropriate. Where the inspecting agent is of known experience and probity, the only danger is likely to exist in connection with his certificate is that of alteration. Unfortunately there are certificates of inspection produced as part of shipping documents in dubious cases, which bear no relationship to the real quality of the goods they purport to describe. Certificates of origin are often a vital part of shipping documents and it might be as well at this stage to deal with their purpose quite briefly. Many countries have variable rates of customs duty depending upon the nature and value of imported goods, whilst others operate preferential rates of duty in favour of particular countries. In order to establish the proper rates (and sometimes whether or not the goods will be allowed in at all) a certificate of origin is essential. Without it, an importer might very well not be allowed to unload his goods. Such certificates may well be part of a set of shipping documents.

An interesting twist to the documentary fraud case came to light during 1979 when the Nigerian banks were obliged to stop sending instructions to pay by telex to other banks around the world, because someone had gained access to their telex system. It is commonplace for a bank, having been put in funds by a client, to send instructions to a corresponding bank elsewhere to pay money against appropriate documents. Clearly, if access is gained to the telex link together with sufficient inside information, banks many thousands of miles away may be instructed to pay against valueless documents. This matter is still under active investigation and, as yet, no satisfactory conclusions have been arrived at which might indicate the scale of the losses involved. However it is believed that the losses to various banks as a result amount to many thousands of pounds.

Charter fraud

Most charterparties are straightforward business arrangements made along well tried lines. Each trade has developed a standard charterparty document suitable for its own purposes so that when a shipper wishes to transport timber from Scandinavia, the charterparty will be a standard form, code named "NUTBALTWOOD," upon which appear conditions appropriate to that particular form of trade. Similarly, a time charter will frequently be evidenced by an agreement code named "TRANSI-TIME" or "BALTIME," and will have standard conditions to which may be added others, or indeed some may be struck out by agreement between the parties. Not all charterers are people with goods to transport because in this as in every other form of commerce, there are opportunities for profit available to the entrepreneur. Most of the recorded maritime frauds in connection with charters are carried out by such people.

The fraudsman has a small business, perhaps a limited company with a very modest share capital and even more modest fixed assets. Knowing that in a depressed economy, shippers will be willing to cut corners and take risks in the hope of reducing transport costs so that their goods can be more attractively priced, he offers transport facilities on a pre-paid freight basis. In times of recession, shipowners whose financial fortunes must always follow those of exporters, will be just as anxious to secure whatever business is available. Given judgement which has been clouded by financial worries, coupled with impressive letter headings and ready answers, it is perhaps understandable that a shipowner may agree to enter into a contract with the fraudsman. Their charterparty will contain clauses which deal with responsibility for port, light and bunkerage charges and it may be that the master will pay as the voyage proceeds, the owner being reimbursed at intervals, and hire for the period will be payable at stated intervals throughout the life of the charter. At this stage, the charterer becomes the disponent owner and has many of the shipowner's powers and rights. We need not concern ourselves with the generality of those rights, suffice it to say that he can deal with shippers as an owner would and need not necessarily reveal to them that his interest in the vessel is only temporary.

The disponent owner, having perhaps paid his first month's hire, may very well trade properly for a period, taking his profits quite legitimately from the freight charged to shippers. There comes a time, however, when he does not pay either hire charges or such other charges as are due from him. Experiences of those who have suffered from the effects of this kind of crime show that the hire charges are usually deferred for one reason or another over a long period. Incidental charges are not met, and the shipowner begins to realise that his disponent owner has no further interest in the ship. This becomes crystal clear when mail is returned from his office unopened, the telephone there is no longer answered and enquiries show the company to have gone out of effective existence. At this stage the defaulting disponent has collected freight on cargo still loaded aboard ship, but has disappeared. The shipowner must do something with the goods aboard his ship and may find himself with substantial bills to meet from port authorities along his ship's last route. Worse, he may find that his ship, not having delivered the cargo to the consignee, has been arrested and thus become central to a protracted and expensive, international legal wrangle.

Until 1970 one might have thought that fraud in connection with the charter by demise, or "bare boat" charter as it is more popularly known, would have been most unlikely. The initial cost of chartering a ship in this way is high, because the disponent owner undertakes from the very beginning to pay for a crew, bunkering and all the usual expenses associated with full-blooded ownership. Now, however, there is no such certainty because it is becoming clear that the scale of maritime crime is much higher than was believed, and that there are funds available to finance fraud on a massive scale.

Scuttling Fraud

A much used alternative to this heading is the "rust bucket" fraud, which describes most vessels that became a casualty as a result of being deliberately sunk. With the occasional exception, these crimes are committed by ship-owners, and those owners fall into a clearly definable category. The essence of the fraud lies in a situation where a ship is approaching or has passed the end of its economic life, taking into account age, condition and the prevailing freight market. The crime can be aimed at the hull and its insurers alone, or against both hull and cargo.

It is quite well known among those who have suffered loss, and among those whose task it is to investigate suspicious losses, that there is no difficulty in obtaining men prepared to scuttle ships at a price. A dishonest owner will either pay his own crew a sum to scuttle the ship during the course of a voyage, or alternatively, will hire a different crew whose task will be to sink the vessel. Divers can only operate effectively at relatively shallow depths, whereas in the oceans there are deeps or trenches whose floor is far beyond reach by ordinary means. It is usually into one of these inaccessible areas that a scuttled ship will settle but, if the scuttling crew are unable to reach a suitable place, the ship's position will be falsified in the casualty report. In any event the ship will be beyond investigation. Scuttling implies that the ship is deliberately sunk perhaps by explosives or some other method. Equally effective and just as difficult to prove are those instances where a ship's destruction is achieved by arson. An advantage to the criminal in arson cases is that the vessel need not even be at sea, providing of course that the port in which the "accident" occurs has no efficient fire fighters, and a fierce enough fire will often destroy evidence of its origin.

The prerequisites for a successful scuttling fraud are, then, a vessel subject to an insurance policy, men prepared to destroy the vessel and a dishonest owner. How, then may potentially defrauding ship-owners be identified, because it is of some importance to insurance and cargo interests to be able to do so. An analysis of casualties known or suspected to have been deliberately scuttled shows that with the outstanding exception, they are the property of very small operators and sail under a flag of convenience. Thus if one wanted to draw up a specification for a scuttling fraud, one would specify a vessel of 15 or more years, owned by a single ship company based in a tax haven country sailing under a flag of convenience and with a Greek, Asian or oriental crew. Having suggested an archetypal fraudsman drawn from past experience, one must not lose sight of the possibility, indeed, in view of the fate of a supertanker in January 1980, the certainty of a much wider spread of crimes involving destruction of vessels.

It will have been noted that nothing has been said in the discussion on scuttling, about cargoes lost with scuttled and burned ships. Almost always there will be concurrent loss of cargo but this facet is covered by the next section on cargo thefts.

Cargo theft

By cargo theft, is not meant the kind of pilferage that was an inherent part of port life before containerisation, and still is to a degree. Within the scope of this book, cargo theft means misappropriation of the whole or a substantial part of a ship's cargo to the eventual detriment of insurers. Scuttling frauds are seldom carried out simply to raise money on the disposal of an unwanted hull, but will include, for the perpetrator, an additional profit from whatever cargo was aboard. Sometimes shipowner and shipper are one and the same. A successful fraud nets the criminal insurance on both hull and cargo, with an added bonus of the value of the cargo which was secretly landed before scuttling.

Cargo thefts not associated with scuttling can be carried out in a multitude of ways, of which examples abound in insurance office files. Once again the thefts will be more likely to happen during periods of recession and with small operators whose single ship tramps under a flag of convenience to wherever its cargo is supposed to take it. The reality sometimes is that the cargo does not arrive at its port of destination. Take, for example, a dishonest owner who has loaded valuable cargo of a kind much desired in some middle eastern country. Having issued bills of lading and sailed, ostensibly for the consignee's nominated port, the ship is then diverted to a place where cargo may be discharged and sold on the quayside. A rapid change of name, effected with paint pot and brush, and the ship is off again for its next adventure. If necessary to avoid potential trouble, a change of flag will often be made whilst still at sea and thus *SS. ABC* of Panama becomes overnight the *SS. DEF* of Nicosia.

In an uncomplicated case of cargo theft where cargo was despatched c.i.f., the eventual loser as in most maritime crime, will be the insurers. However there will frequently be incidental losses to consignees who hold the insurable interest, not least of all through loss of trading profits arising due to absence of the goods with which they intended to deal.

This brief review of maritime crimes should be regarded as a mere outline of crimes possible to classify under the four suggested headings. The list cannot be considered closed, nor should it be believed that no new classifications may arise in the future. Although there will be a strong element of one kind of crime in any given situation, there will almost certainly be elements of one or more others as well. A documentary credit fraud will usually involve loss of cargo by theft, a scuttling fraud will usually involve theft as either a primary or secondary object and may also be aided in its commission by false documents of one kind or another. Chartering frauds will sometimes include both document and theft classification in some measure when an analysis of the crime is made. By no means unlikely is the maritime fraud which encompasses charter, documents, theft and scuttling in equal measure, which proves that even the broad method of classification used is necessarily limited in completeness. Finally, one ought to consider crime in the context of the massive increase in container traffic.

Containerisation

Containerisation has brought with it many advantages, and also perhaps more than its share of crime problems. Quite apart from its own peculiar brand of theft, the container lends itself to fraud and deception. When an international organisation is shipping from "self to self" it has every opportunity to fake evidence of interference in transit and gain insurance benefit for a shortage which was either an underloading at the point of origin or an under-declaration of outturn at the point of receipt.

This type of malpractice need not be restricted to the self/self operation. Two documented cases show variations on this theme. On one, on an apparent shortage on outturn, the consignor reported the loading of a volume of stock which was greater than the capacity of the container. When this discrepancy was pointed out the consignor "discovered" a tally error at the point of loading, which meant there was no crime. In another case a company was acting as warehouse and forwarding agent for a manufacturer. On hearing that the manufacturer was to take the operation over himself in the near future the forwarder short-loaded the next container he delivered and held stock back to cover shortages in the goods still in his warehouse. What he failed to realise was that the shortages were due to theft and the stock stolen from the warehouse had been recovered by the police, so that he was claiming that more stock existed than had ever been manufactured.

Consequences not merely financial may well result from other malpractices with containers. In order to save on freight rates which might otherwise be surcharged some companies have been known to underdeclare the contents of containers presented for shipping. Underdeclaration of weight will only cause stowage problems, but failure to declare the hazardous nature of contents could well cause a catastrophe at sea.

Even the State can fall victim to fraudulent use of the container. Some countries have very strict exchange-control regulations in order to protect their economy. These regulations create difficulties and in at least one area, containerisation has provided a method of circumventing them. The system requires a measure of international conspiracy. The importer will order and pay by letter of credit for a certain quantity of goods. The exporter will prepare all documentation and pay freight and all charges for the quantity ordered, but will supply only, say, one-tenth of the quantity. The cover afforded by the container will disguise this fact. When the container reaches its port of destination it will wait for customs clearance until the consignee calls for delivery—and it only remains for him to arrange to steal his own container in the meantime. In some countries this is a comparatively simple operation. As will be seen, although the incidental costs of the theft of the container and the expenses incurred by the importer have to be paid, the operation not only produces the insurance money for the claim on the non-existent cargo but also achieves its primary objective of getting money out of the country.

Outside the classification of fraud is another form of maritime crime: piracy. The law of piracy, with its difficulties, is now considered but some recent examples and the climate in which they are committed is of some interest. The climate is a political one, because one sees that acts of piracy are common, and indeed only likely in association with nations whose political condition is unstable.

Piracy may at first sight appear to be a crime of purely historical interest, but nothing could be further from the truth as the events of recent years and months have clearly demonstrated. The so-called boat people, unfortunate refugees from the war-torn Far East who, sailing in their flimsy boats to find a measure of peace, found instead pirates who are every bit as cruel and avaricious as those of fiction. The "boat people" carried their wealth in the form of gold and were, in consequence, the natural targets of sea-borne robbers. Of course it is also true to say that they were victims of fraudsmen long before they were intercepted by pirates, for many of them paid over large proportions of their wealth to unscrupulous men who were prepared to pack them into unsafe vessels with insufficient supplies, leaving them to the mercies of the sea.

They were not the only victims of piracy during 1979 and 1980 as a study of contemporary news reports will show. In October 1979 for example, the Guardian newspaper was reporting piratical attacks on shipping in Lebanese waters with four cases discovered in under a month. Cuban refugees in 1980, departing unlawfully from their homeland in an attempt to reach the United States of America, found themselves in a similar plight. In November 1979, the United Nations held a conference in London during which piracy figured importantly in an agenda aimed at combating all forms of international maritime crime. In the same year the Honourable Mr. Justice G.S.M. Green, Chief Justice of Tasmania addressed a meeting of the Maritime Law Association of Australia and New Zealand on the same subject. He was able to illustrate his address with a number of recent cases, many of which involved loss of life.

Before considering the law on piracy, however, it might be of advantage to look briefly at a crime called barratry. There is no such crime in British criminal law under that name but a useful definition of the word can be found in various dictionaries, illustrating that it serves to describe most maritime crime with the exception of piracy.

Barratry

"In commerce, any fraud committed by the master or mariners of a ship whereby the owners, insurers or shippers are injured; as by deviation from the proper course of the voyage by the captain for his own private purposes; fraudulent negligence; theft of any part of the cargo, etc." (*British Encyclopaedia*, 1933.)

For those readers whose interest is general rather than strictly of a technical legal nature, the term piracy can happily include crimes which fall more accurately under the definition of barratry. For those who prefer, or are obliged to be more precise, piracy will require a somewhat more extensive discussion.

Piracy

The law of piracy has a particular difficulty for those who need to consider it, because it must be examined in two separate contexts, namely as an international crime and as one of a domestic nature. The first, *piracy jure gentium* concerns piratical acts against international laws to which a large number of states subscribe, the second is found in statutes enacted by individual nations seeking to contain crimes committed within their own jurisdiction. Regrettably, international law and domestic laws are not in agreement as to a proper definition of piracy so that an act committed outside the territorial jurisdiction of a particular nation might be piracy as defined by international law, yet not be so within the domestic law of that nation.

The different approach is well illustrated by the definition contained in international and British criminal laws.

International law

The Convention on the High Seas, signed at Geneva in 1958, defined piracy in Article 15 in the following terms:

> "Piracy consists of the following acts:
>
> (1) Any illegal acts of violence, detention or depredation, committed for private ends by the crew or the passengers of a private ship or a private aircraft, and directed:
>> (a) on the high seas, against another ship or aircraft, or against persons or property on board such ship or aircraft;
>> (b) against a ship, aircraft or persons or property in a place outside the jurisdiction of any state;
>
> (2) Any act of voluntary participation in the operation of a ship or aircraft with knowledge of facts making it a pirate ship or aircraft;
>
> (3) Any act of inciting or of intentionally facilitating an act described in sub-paragraph (1) or (2) of this article."

Article 16:

> "The acts of piracy as defined in article 15, committed by a warship, government ship or aircraft whose crew has mutinied and taken control of the ship or aircraft are assimilated to acts committed by a private ship."

Article 17:

> "A ship or aircraft is considered a pirate ship or aircraft if it is intended by the persons in dominant control to be used for the purpose of committing one of the acts referred to in article 15. The same applied if the ship or aircraft has been used to commit such act so long as it remains under the control of the persons guilty of that act."

These articles have been adopted as part of British domestic law, having been made so by the Tokyo Convention Act 1967. The broad effect of this is that where the British authorities take those who offend against articles 15–17 into custody, they may try them in British courts of law, providing the crime was committed on the high seas or where the Admiralty courts have jurisdiction.

Domestic law

Before the adoption of the Geneva Convention articles, British domestic laws were contained in ancient statutes dating from the

Piracy Act 1698 to the Slave Trade Act 1824. The first of these defines piracy in the romantic schoolboy adventure mode, whilst the second declares that trading in slaves is piracy and will attract the penalties of that condition.

Piracy Act 1698, s.8.   This section defines piracy at length but for present purposes, an edited version of its provisions will be sufficient. Broadly, the acts constituting piracy are: Within the Admiralty jurisdiction, a master or mariner betraying trust and turning pirate, enemy or rebel, and, unlawfully, running away with ship, armaments, or cargo or turning them over to pirates. Bringing seducing messages from pirates, corrupting or attempting to corrupt master or mariners to run away with or yield up ship, etc., to pirates. Preventing the master from defending his ship, etc., from pirates, or making a revolt in the ship.

Piracy Act 1837, s.2.   Whosoever, with intent to commit or at the time or immediately before or immediately after committing the crime of piracy in respect of any ship or vessel, shall assault, with intent to murder, any person being on board or belonging to such ship or vessel, or shall stab, cut or wound any such person or unlawfully do any act, by which the life of such person may be endangered, shall be guilty of an offence, and being convicted thereof, shall suffer death. (Amended to life imprisonment).

From these definitions, one can see that to recognise piracy with any degree of certainty can be a difficult exercise. This difficulty is made more so when terrorism is involved in what appear to be piratical acts, because then it cannot be said that the acts complained of are for private ends, but rather for political purposes in the interests of a wider community. When such is the case, the definition of piracy in international law is of only marginal assistance. It has been said that the Convention from which articles 15–17 sprang did little to help in the control of piracy, in no matter what form, but instead rendered it a dead letter since a true basis for a nation to find jurisdiction would be rare. Not only does article 15 require the act complained of to be for private ends, but it also requires it to be directed against another vessel or aircraft, thus effectively removing any form of passenger or crew hijacking from the definition of piracy.

For an analysis of the concepts of fraud and misrepresentation, which are at the heart of most maritime crimes (with the exception of piracy), see the paper by Lord Hacking, "Protection under the common law against fraud and misrepresentation," given at the Second International Seminar on the Prevention of Shipping Fraud, reprinted in Appendix F.

5 Maritime Crimes Examined

Documentary Frauds

Despite the advantages of instant communication and computerised accountancy, shipping is still beset with documentary frauds. Often the culprits can rely on port and bank officials to accept without question forged papers or to neglect routine checks that are intended to save the innocent from financial loss. Because ships, unlike aircraft, take weeks rather than hours to reach destinations, the criminals have time to cover their tracks.

If the victim is able to seek justice in a western court, the law can be slow. But in countries where the legal system is still evolving, and with the guilty party beyond reach, the innocent can find themselves the targets of revenge.

There have been two such examples in recent years. One concerns the Greek motor vessel, the *Lord Byron*; the other, a shipment of groundnuts from one African country to another.

(1)   *The Lord Byron*

The ill-fated journey of this 6,549 gross-tonner started in August 1974. Although owned by Valia Oceanica Armadora S.A. of Piraeus, she was managed by Condaras (Hellas) Ltd. S.A., who in June 1974 had arranged a 12-month time charter to Schellen Shipping and Chartering Company Ltd. of Rotterdam. It was the Dutch company which in good faith sub-chartered her to a concern called Consolidated Cosmopolitan Lines of Bangkok, Thailand, for a single voyage from South East Asia to East Africa.

The *Lord Byron* reached Bangkok on September 8 where she stood idle until Saturday, September 21. Shortly before midnight some barges came alongside loaded with 6,874 bags of sugar which the Greek ship took aboard. It was almost six the next morning before the task was finished. Because it was both a Sunday and an early hour, the charterer's agent, Eastern Development Corporation, told the master, Captain Nicholas Michalopoulos, that neither bill of lading nor manifest could be handed to him but that these would be forwarded to the port of discharge. There was nothing unusual about this and after signing a mate's receipt for the 6,874 bags containing 687 tons of sugar, he sailed on instruction to Singapore to load some timber. The sugar was for Berbera, Somali Democratic Republic, and the timber for the Yemen. Michalopoulos reached Berbera on October 10 and discharged the cargo of sugar. Then port authorities refused to allow him, his crew and his ship to leave.

The reason, they explained, was that he should have brought 10,000 tons of sugar which the Somali Government had not only ordered, but paid for. They further accused him of having off-loaded some of the sugar at another port and tried to get him to sign a confession to that effect. Michalopoulos refused, pointing out that a ship with a cargo capacity of only 8,200 tons could hardly carry 2,400 tons of timber and 10,000 tons of sugar.

Attempts by the time charterers to release the *Lord Byron* were hampered by the Somali authorities, who prevented direct communication with the ship's master. They immediately asked Drew and Napier, the Protection and Indemnity Club Singapore representatives, to instigate enquiries in the Far East.

It transpired that in 1973 and 1974 East Africa was hit by a severe drought. With its own sugar crop stricken, Somalia was forced to look for alternative supplies. The Somali Government's National Agency of Commerce made it known that it was in the market for 10,000 tons of sugar at the lowest possible tender. It operated through the offices of Haji M.S.Mohidin and Sons of Mombasa who in turn detailed a Kenyan with Somali origins named A.M.Hatimi to make inquiries. Hatimi was put in touch with Crescent Impex (Pte) Ltd. of 39 Guan Street, Singapore, who opened negotiations with a Chinaman named Chern Chernratanarak of Eastern Development Corporation of Bangkok, known to everyone as "Mr. Chern". He was a director of six other companies.

Chern died in Bangkok in 1975, but despite the existence of a death certificate, the police and several lawyers are looking for him concerning rice and sugar smuggling allegations. They believe that the report of his death is false.

His involvement with the sugar deal dates back to May 1974 when he agreed to supply the Somalis with the 10,000 tons for 5.9 million U.S. dollars. Chern asked the purchasers to open a letter of credit for the account of another Singapore company, Australia S.E.A. Holdings (Pte) Ltd. which had been created only two weeks previously with a capital of a mere two U.S. dollars, and whose directors were Chin Coh Seng and Grace Florence May Chin. Chin was a professor of accountancy and business administration at Singapore University. Crescent Impex was later to claim that lacking experience of such a large operation as the sugar deal, they sought Chin's advice. Australia S.E.A. Holdings was his brainchild and was formed with the full approval of Crescent Impex's directors, who were the professor's wife and brother.

The new company opened an account with the Moscow Narodny Bank Ltd. of Singapore and it was this account that was named in the Somali letter of credit for the 5.9 million U.S. dollars. Among the documents presented when the money was claimed was a bill of lading headed "C.C. Line," which stood for Consolidated Cosmopolitan Line, with We Hua Trading Company Ltd. named as the agents. We Hua was later found to be a company of which Chern was a director. The bill of lading stated that Australia S.E.A. Holdings had loaded 100,000 new jute bags containing a total of 10,000 tons of sugar aboard the *MS Delwind*—not the *Lord Byron*—at Koh-Si-Cheng, a small island near Bangkok, for delivery to the National Agency of Commerce, Berbera. This document was presented on June 24, 1974, and the 5.9 million U.S. dollars were collected on July 11. The Somalis later claimed that this bill, together with the certificate of origin, the chemical analysis and other documents, were all signed by Professor Chin.

In the Somali sugar saga the *Delwind* could almost be described as "the ship that never was" although she certainly existed. But she was not in the vicinity of Bangkok on June 24. Owned by the Thai Ship Company of Hong Kong, she sailed from Vancouver on May 14 with a load of grain which she discharged at Osaka on May 29, went into dry dock on June 13 and was sold about this time to an Italian company who changed her name to *Span Seconda*. She went on to Bangkok under her new name, arriving there on August 23 and left in ballast for Vancouver the same day.

In October 1974 there were two incidents that gave the lie to the claim that the sugar had been despatched to Somalia. On the 23rd the We Hua Trading Company telegraphed the Moscow Narodny Bank that the sugar was still in their go-downs and on the 31st P.K.Hogan of Crescent Impex signed a statement that he visited and inspected the cargo intended for the *Delwind* in two go-downs containing 3,000 tons each and a third containing 2,000 tons; a rainstorm prevented him inspecting the balance.

The background to the *Lord Byron*'s involvement was an approach by Professor Chin "on behalf of a Mr. Chern of Bangkok" to a Singapore chartering broker named Krikke of Cosmar F.E. (Pte) Ltd. This resulted in the Greek ship being chartered for the account of Consolidated Cosmopolitan Lines from Schellan of Holland. The charter party was signed by Van Ommeren of London on C.C. Line's behalf. And so the *Lord Byron* found itself at Bangkok on September 8.

Shortly after this, although the date is not established, Eastern Development Corporation is alleged by the Berbera port authorities to have sent them a telegram to the effect that the merchant vessel *Lord Byron* had transshipped 687 tons of sugar from the *Delwind* at Nicobar Island in the Indian Ocean. The port authorities also claim to have in their possession a mate's receipt for 687 tons of sugar, with the word Bangkok cancelled and replaced with "Nicobar Island."

As soon as Schellen, the Dutch time-charterers, heard about the *Lord Byron*'s detention, they tried to contact Captain Michalopoulos, but with communications blocked and visas refused, they were unable to gain entry. The Dutch Government, however, immediately sent a special envoy to Somalia. He was a Mr. W. Bertens who was eventually permitted to visit the *Lord Byron*. He reached Berbera on December 14, 1974, and started his enquiries but later said he was baffled by a telegram Michalopoulos was alleged to have sent to the Berbera port authorities on September 8, but which he denied, stating that "SS Delwind could not reach Maldive and have now anchored near Nicobar is all cargo aboard safe but shifting of cargo into my vessel slow stop ETA Berbera reverting stop Master stop Lord Byron."

Bertens returned to Mogadishu on December 16 where he discussed the whole affair with the Somali Foreign Trade Minister Ahmed Mohamed Mohamud. The minister presented his ultimatum: his government required the sugar for which it had paid, or its current value, otherwise the *Lord Byron* would not be allowed to sail. On December 23, Bertens saw the legal adviser to the Somali Revolutionary Council, Addillahi Sai Osman, who told him bluntly that normal international practice was of no consequence if it conflicted with Somali interests. In other words, possession of the *Lord Byron* gave them a strong bargaining lever. Bertens pleaded but it was quite clear that with all the publicity the affair had received, the Somalis were not going to back down without getting something back. He left Somalia on Christmas Day.

While Bertens was involved in Somalia, John Condaras, a director of the Greek managing company which had arranged the original charter to Schellen, flew to Bangkok and Singapore in an attempt to unravel the mystery. He then flew on to Khartoum to see the Greek Ambassador who was also accredited to the Somali Democratic Republic. Despite approaches to Somali diplomatic missions in Beirut, Cairo and Rome, no visas to Somalia were forthcoming for Condaras or anyone from his company.

Condaras and his staff persevered and after repeated applications, Condaras himself was able to get a visa from the Somali mission in Brussels, while A.I. Tzamtzis, the company's port captain, managed to obtain one for himself while on a visit to Jedda, Saudi Arabia, where he was trying to arrange provisions for the *Lord Byron*'s trapped crew.

The two men linked up and flew into Mogadishu on January 29, 1975, where they saw the Somali Foreign Trade Minister who repeated his demands: 10,000 tons of sugar or its current price; otherwise no ship. The *Lord Byron,* he claimed, had participated in a swindle against his government, but he conceded that this could have happened without the ship's company being aware of it. It took considerable argument to persuade the Somali authorities to grant an entry visa for the Protection and Indemnity Club lawyer, Ian Maclachlan, who needed to collect all relevant facts. There was further hedging when permission was sought for all three men to visit Berbera; it was argued that as the ship's crew were free to circulate and were in good health, there was no need for the two Greeks to make the trip.

Eventually the Minister for Foreign Trade granted permission on the understanding that all discussions with the crew were in English and in the presence of the police and of lawyers acting for the police and the agents. Condaras and Tzamtzis went to Berbera without waiting for Maclachlan. Despite the minister's claim, they found that the ship's crew were only allowed ashore during daylight and could not travel outside the town. They were suffering shortages which the supplies from Jedda only partly alleviated.

As agreed, all interviews took place in English and in the presence of police and lawyers. The master denied having been involved in any swindle at any time and pointed out that he had in fact delivered the sugar stipulated on the mate's receipt. The two men returned to Mogadishu to find that there was still no entry visa for the P and I Club lawyer. They thus found themselves involved in further arguments and pleadings. Only after still more frustrating delays did the authorities change their minds. Maclachlan received his visa on February 10 and reached Somalia the next day. He and the two Greek shipping men met the Foreign Trade Minister and the Governor of the Commercial Bank of Somalia on the 15th.

The Governor had returned from Bangkok and Singapore where he had headed a five-man Somali investigation team. After 50 days they had achieved little, beyond concluding that their country had been victimised by Chern, assisted by corrupt officials in Thailand. The Somalis then argued that as managers of the *Lord Byron*, the Condaras organisation should exert pressure on the governments of Greece, Holland, the United Kingdom and Singapore to assist Somalia in getting compensation. But when it was suggested that on their part, the Somali authorities should release the ship and her crew, there was adamant refusal. Again the terms were outlined: there must be either 10,000 tons of sugar delivered to Berbera or 5.9 million U.S. dollars. The *Lord Byron* would otherwise remain in Somali hands. Further, there could be no movement or even replacement of crew "for the time being."

Unable to see any glimmer of light at the end of the tunnel, the dejected visitors left Somalia. Meanwhile, Drew and Napier, the two P and I Club representatives, were making more progress than had the Somali investigators in Bangkok and Singapore. They discovered that the company which issued the bill of lading, Consolidated Cosmopolitan Lines, had never really existed under that name. Nor was there proof that the 10,000 tons of sugar, supposed to be stored in three Bangkok go-downs, had existed either.

According to Thai law, only two companies, Thailand Sugar Corporation and Suko, possessed standing authority to export sugar. Anyone else required a special licence and none had been issued in connection with any Somali shipment. Also, exports could only be handled by Thai shippers; foreign companies, such as the Singapore based Australia S.E.A. Holdings, were barred from doing so.

They also found that a bill of lading issued on June 24, 1974, recorded that the sugar had been loaded on the *Delwind,* but as we know this ship did not reach Bangkok for another 60 days—on August 23—by which time she had been renamed *Span Seconda* and she left without taking on any cargo.

Another factor that pointed to the irregularity of the operation was that although the sugar merchants were in Thailand, the letter of credit was opened for an account in Singapore. Drew and Napier concluded that Australia S.E.A. Holdings was created only to cash the letter of credit and to be named as the shippers. They were reinforced in this belief when they established that Professor Chin, the founder of this company, signed all the documents needed to cash the letter of credit—bill of lading, certificate of origin, certificate of analysis and certificate of quantity and quality. The picture was emerging that there had never been any intention of supplying Somalia with 10,000 tons of sugar in exchange for the 5.9 million U.S. dollars, that the *Delwind* was chosen as a convenient name to enter on the forged documents in the belief (rightly, as it transpired) that the Somalis would never know that this ship was in dry dock in Japan; that it was only to allay Somali suspicions that the *Lord Byron* was chartered, loaded with a few hundred tons of sugar while a delaying "accident" was staged in Nicobar Island in the hope that the Somalis would believe the rest of the sugar would eventually arrive. Once they had learned what was going on, the Somalis would be expected to release the *Lord Byron,* but part of the confidence trick was to involve her—hence the forged telegram Michalopoulos was supposed to have sent to the Berbera port authorities on September 8. Whether or not the Somalis suspected that this was a forgery, its possession gave them the "evidence" they needed to brand the *Lord Byron* as part of the scheme to defraud their government. They had lost nearly 6 million U.S. dollars, and someone was going to pay. Whether it was Chin or Chern, the owners or managers of the *Lord Byron* or an insurance company did not matter.

With so much weighing against them, Condaras (Hellas) Ltd. S.A.

felt they had reached an impasse, but they continued to battle for the release of the master and crew, even though they saw little immediate chance of getting their ship back. Tzamtzis made a further visit to Mogadishu on April 26, 1975, but it was when he called again on May 31 that a breakthrough came. The Somalis were prepared to release the crew, but not the master. Michalopoulos, the Government insisted, must remain to give evidence at a forthcoming trial—only later did it transpire that he was to be a defendant. The crew left for home on June 12.

The Somalis were busy preparing their case against the *Lord Byron* and her master. On September 29, Tzamtzis returned to Mogadishu to review the situation, finding that Michalopoulos had been moved there from Berbera and was staying in a hotel. After contacting a possible local defence lawyer, Robleh Mariano, Tzamtzis flew to Berbera and carried out a survey of the *Lord Byron,* assisted by an engineer. He returned to Athens on October 12 to brief his employers and flew again to Somalia on November 23 with the P and I Club Middle East representative, Dr. Mustafa El Hefnaoui. On this visit Mariano was officially commissioned to prepare the defence and taken to Athens for discussions.

The trial opened in February 1976 before a security court at Mogadishu. John Condaras, Tzamtzis and El Hefnaoui sat through the proceedings. Three others—John Perakis (legal adviser to the managing company), Pannir Selvam, a Singapore lawyer who conducted investigations in the Far East, and Mr. E. Tzaferis, the Greek Ambassador to Somalia who lived in Khartoum—arrived but left when the trial was suddenly postponed for four days. Owing to pressure of other business, they were unable to return.

When the case eventually opened, the attorney general claimed that the *Lord Byron* and her master were involved in a six million U.S. dollar fraud directed against the Somali economy, but the real crime, he alleged, was bigger than the one they were now hearing. The charges against Michalopoulos alleged his involvement in "a false telegram" and his failure to deliver the bill of lading and cargo manifest. The master pleaded not guilty.

Mariano, for the defence, said that there was no case to answer. He pointed out that the laws which the master was supposed to have violated applied only to exports from Somalia, and that any infringement of them must be committed within the country or territorial waters. The president said that this aspect would be considered later (in the end it apparently carried no weight) but that meanwhile the trial would continue. Witnesses called for the prosecution included the head of the Somali shipping agency, Berbera's port captain and some members of the abortive investigation team sent to the Far East under the Bank governor.

Only one defence witness was called; one of the same Somali investigation team. He admitted that the person acting in a liaison capacity between the Somali Government and the shippers was a Somali with Kenyan citizenship. This evidence was omitted from the trial transcript later produced by the Somalis. Although it was not mentioned in court, investigations made by Pannir Selvam, the Singapore lawyer, suggest that this individual received 1.5 million U.S. dollars for his part in the sugar deal.

Having taken the oath, Michalopoulos, *Lord Byron*'s master, told the court that he acted according to instructions given by the shippers and the normal practices of the shipping business. His orders were to load cargoes in Bangkok and Singapore for Berbera and Hodeidah. The quantity of the cargo, he explained, was determined solely by the local agent who was also acting as the shipper. It was he who had promised that the documents would be mailed to the port of discharge, and this was common practice, particularly where the loading had been completed on a Sunday.

The attorney general insisted that Captain Michalopoulos had taken part in a fraudulent act against the Somali people. He asked for a sentence of four years in prison. The ship's owners, he said, should be fined three times the value of the missing sugar—a total in the region of 18 million U.S. dollars—and until the fine was paid the *Lord Byron* should remain in Berbera. If the payment was not made, the ship should be presented to those to whom the sugar or the payment was due.

Mariano refuted these arguments by claiming that not only had no crime been committed in Somalia or its territorial waters but that the trial was in contravention of the 1958 Geneva Maritime Convention. He submitted that if a crime had been committed, it was covered by a Supreme Revolutionary Council amnesty of 1975 and further, that it was the shippers alone who had swindled the Somali Government. They had done so by depositing a bill of lading three months before the *Lord Byron* was chartered.

The defence counsel reminded the court that it was the Moscow Narodny Bank in Singapore which had cashed the letter of credit without even checking the validity of the bill of lading and other documents. In the circumstances the court would have no alternative but to declare his client innocent. There could be no question of a fine and the master and his ship should be released immediately.

The president said that the court would consider the evidence and announce its verdict at a later sitting, the date of which would be given to all interested parties in advance. It was almost eight weeks later that a telex message reached the Condaras offices in Greece. Dated April 9, 1976, it was from Mariano. It announced that Captain Michalopoulos had been sentenced to four years imprisonment and the *Lord Byron* fined 5.9 million U.S. dollars, the vessel to be seized and sold by public auction on non-payment of the fine. Condaras learned from other sources that Michalopoulos had been removed to prison.

The master served only nine months before being released under an amnesty, but on his return to Athens he died in hospital from heart failure. The *Lord Byron* was forcibly held at Berbera until late 1979—a total of five years—before being released, by which time it was necessary to tow her home to Greece.

Whatever the logic that went into official Somali thinking, whatever the sympathy that must be felt for a small nation being so deliberately defrauded, the legality of what followed was, by any standards, wholly wrong. It revealed a lack of business acumen by the Somali Government whose responsible officials had failed to investigate the financial standing of the company which cashed the letter of credit for nearly 6 million U.S. dollars—a company which at the time had only just been created with a mere two dollars capital. With a prohibition on foreign companies exporting sugar from Thailand, it is surprising that no responsible person questioned the transfer of the letter of credit from Bangkok to Singapore. Even more surprising was the failure of any interested party to investigate the background of the company issuing the bill of lading.

The Somali Government displayed extraordinary lethargy in the arrangements it made for a team of investigators to visit the Far East. By the time a team, headed by the Governor of the Commercial Bank, was sent, five months had passed since the letter of credit had been cashed, and their 50 days of probing met with no success.

The governor told a meeting of Condaras executives and Ministry of Commerce officials on February 15, 1975 that he had met Chern in Bangkok. This was confirmed in a letter by Hatimi, the link man, in a letter to Selvam, the P and I Club lawyer, dated May 7, 1975. Yet at a further meeting with the managing company executives and Mariano, their lawyer, on the day of the trial, the Governor related how he had tried to telephone Chern but was told he was at a meeting with some general. The news "was enough" to make him (the Governor) leave Thailand.

Another puzzling aspect is the Governor's description of the link man Hatimi, whom he said he had met in Singapore, as an honest man. Yet he expressed surprise when told that the Kenyan citizen had apparently received a commission of 1.5 million U.S. dollars for arranging the sugar deal.

The investigating committee's report on its 50 days in the Far East was never shown to the managing company although Condaras gave the Somalis access to all the evidence he had in his possession.

A suspicious factor is that the court's decision was issued on a Friday (April 9, 1976)—the Muslim day of rest. Every Thursday the Supreme Revolutionary Council of Somalia meets. Was the verdict discussed at its meeting on April 8 and was it therefore political rather than judicial? For the Somalis singularly failed to produce any evidence that would have convicted the *Lord Byron* and her master in a normal Western court. Condaras and his associates can be forgiven for believing that an innocent man was imprisoned and an innocent ship seized for political ends.

Part of the mystery of the whole affair is the background of "Mr Chern" (Chern Chernratanarak). Inquiries made by the Condaras company show that he was jailed on several occasions over charges relating to dishonoured cheques, while outstanding claims against him range from unpaid charter hires to falsification of documents.

At the time of the *Lord Byron* arrest he was described as being in his early to mid-forties and married with a small son. Condaras are in possession of a copy of his death certificate, which states that he died from cancer of the pancreas on May 29, 1975, in Bangkok, but many people who knew him said they felt that he always looked too fit to be suffering from such a debilitating illness. At the time of his "death" the police had warrants out for his arrest in connection with alleged rice and sugar smuggling deals. His own staff claimed that he was abroad but it was also reported that one of his offices had been destroyed by fire and with it a number of documents. Factors that persuaded the Greek company that he could be alive were the refusal by his lawyer to confirm his death, the quiet nature of his funeral—it lacked the normal Chinese traditional mourning ceremonies—and reports that he had been seen in Djakarta later in the year. A Thai policeman who had once arrested him claims to have spotted him driving in Bangkok on December 11, 1975. Attempts to have the body exhumed were refused.

(2) *The Angolan groundnuts fraud*

The Angolan documentary fraud case dates from the latter part of 1976 when Angola decided to import groundnuts for its oil extract-ing industry. The government agency Central Angolana de Importacao (or Importang) contacted a 44-year-old Portuguese merchant with Angolan connections—the country had been a Portuguese colony for four centuries until gaining independence in 1975. He was Manuel Jose Pires, manager of Sociedade Industrial e Exportadora Rimalpi Limitada (Rimalpi) of Lisbon, and he agreed to supply 13,420 tons of "dehulled groundnuts suitable for the extrac-tion of oil," c.i.f. Luanda and Lobito for 6,844,200. U.S. dollars.

Pires asked for payment to be made through the Union Bank of Switzerland against shipping documents which he would produce.

Importang instructed the Bank of Angola to open documentary credit with the Swiss bank. The letter of credit was dated December 14, 1976, and was valid until January 31, 1977. The bank was instructed to pay the money only on production of an invoice in quintuplicate, insurance policy covering various risks including total loss and war, certificate of origin, certificate of weight and quantity, bills of lading, clean on board papers, certificate of quality and analysis and a certificate of packing issued by an internationally recognised organisation.

Pires seemed to be in no hurry to arrange the shipment, for he persuaded the Angolans to extend the credit period to February 15, then to March 5 and eventually to April 15, 1977, and to change the specification of the cargo to "groundnuts without shells."

He had by then contacted Doraldo Perriera Lima, owner of Lima Navigation Limited, a shipping company registered in Bermuda but operating from Hamburg. Not owning ships himself, Lima used vessels on time charter. The documents eventually presented to the Swiss bank bore the names of two such ships—the *Pistis* and the *Saronicos Gulf*, both Greek owned.

The officials of the Union Bank of Switzerland saw that the documents for the *Pistis* certified a shipment of 57,401 bags of groundnuts without shells with a gross weight of 4,420 tons, loaded at Beira, Mozambique, and destined for the Angolan ports of Luanda and Lobito. They carried the seal of Lima's Hamburg office and a signature said to be that of Lima's Beira agent. The documents for the *Saronicos Gulf* certified 116,885 bags of groundnuts without shells weighing 9,000 tons, also loaded at Beira for Luanda and Lobito.

Having identified the documents, the Zurich bank officials were obliged to pay unless they suspected anything amiss. Had the bankers seen that day's Lloyd's List, they would have noticed that one of the two ships was in dry dock in Khalkis, Greece, and the other actually at Luanda—and not just outside Beira on its way around the Cape—where it was discharging a general cargo.

The money was paid over to Lima on April 18. In Angola the weeks dragged by as Importang awaited the arrival of the nuts. Meanwhile on May 4 the *Pistis,* now out of dry dock, was delivered to the charterers, Lima Navigation, at Lisbon. Her master, Georgios Mavrommatis, says that he was told that he would be loading cargo at Banjul, Senegal, but was to represent that he had taken it aboard at Beira, but that he initially refused. He was then told that if he persisted with this attitude the charter would be revoked.

On June 17, the *Pistis* left Banjul with a cargo, not of groundnuts without shells but of groundnut cake, which is what is left when the oil has been extracted. This, of course, made it quite useless for the purpose the Angolans intended. Mavrommatis was ordered by Lima Navigation to make for the island of Sao Tomé but when no business ensued, was instructed to call at Bonny, Nigeria, then sail to Abidjan and then back to Bonny. It was now August 26.

A cable from the charterers' agent instructed the master to proceed to Luanda but also to open the sealed envelope he had been given in Lisbon and alter the name of the loading port from Beira to Benjul on the enclosed documents. He was not to alter the date of loading—April 17, 1977.

The *Pistis* reached Luanda on August 30. Before he berthed, Mavrommatis was visited by local agents who checked that the changes to the documents had been made. He then tied up and started to discharge, but almost immediately was stopped by port officials. The cargo deception had been spotted. The situation was not eased when an examination of the bill of lading and manifest showed the changes in loading port. Guards were placed on board and the radio room locked. Greece had no representative in Luanda but fortunately the Italian ambassador was prepared to act for them. He came aboard for talks and at first it looked as if the master's difficulties were over. The guards were removed, the radio room unlocked and Lima's agents told him to discharge his general cargo, reload the goundnut cake and make for Sao Tomé and Lisbon. However, permission to sail was withheld and eventually *Pistis* was secured alongside another ship at the pier, guards were again posted and the radio room locked once more.

Meanwhile the *Saronicos Gulf* was sailing towards a similar fate. Captain Christos Terzoglou, of Greece, had joined her in Antwerp in the previous March when she was already on charter to Lima. From then until the end of July she sailed between Bremen, Leixon, Leixos, Sao Tomé, Luanda and Dakar. There she remained until August 11, when instructions arrived for her to make for Banjul. Here, she loaded 3,000 tons of groundnut cake.

Terzoglou reached Dakar on August 16 and took on another 2,885 tons of "cake." He was then presented by the charterers' port captain with a bill of lading showing Beira as the loading port. The master contacted his owners in Greece and was warned that on no account must he sign it. He placed the document in his safe. Later, when able to study it more closely, he noticed several discrepancies in dates, shipments, weights and description of cargo. While at sea he received a cable from Lima ordering him to cross out Beira and substitute Banjul, but decided to ignore this.

On September 20, the *Saronicos Gulf* reached Lobito. Discharging of cargo had barely started when the port authorities instructed Terzoglou to start reloading and troops marched aboard his ship. As has already been stated, there should have been 9,000 tons of groundnuts, but it was quite clear to the importers (Importang) that the ship had not the capacity to carry more than 6,000 tons.

The Angolans complained very bitterly to Pires in Portugal, who in turn passed responsibility to Lima. Pires suggested that as the Angolans were already forcibly holding two of the latter's chartered ships, the *Pistis* and *Saronicos Gulf*, they might as well seize two others that were at that moment in local ports. Thus the *Kalmar* and *Elpis*, like the other two Greek owned, were held.

Those four ships have been hostages since the latter part of 1977. In a civil court judgment handed down in November 1978, payment of 6,844,200 U.S. dollars was demanded, the amount they originally paid for the shipment of groundnuts—not only from the real culprits, Rimalpi, Lima Navigation and the respective heads of these two organisations, but from the Swiss bank and the owners of the seized ships. The court also awarded further sums of 1,865,380 dollars to cover substitute supplies and 870,958 dollas to cover legal fees. The two men, Pires and Lima, are beyond the jurisdiction of the Angolan court and the reach of everyone else concerned in this case. Lima was last heard of in Brazil and no one is sure where Pires is.

The Angolan government, perhaps quite understandably, fell into the trap of attempting to obtain its needs at the lowest possible price. But of course they attempted to do so in a situation where fraud can flourish almost unchecked. In a spirit of frustration, they then seized ships owned by innocent parties and thus caused them great inconvenience and financial loss. Actions of this kind, no less than the initial crime committed against the Angolan government, cause great concern to the maritime nations and to those whose business it is to provide ships for the world's trade.

Cargo Frauds

A growing form of maritime fraud involves cargo, often ordered and paid for by a Third World customer, which after being loaded onto a ship destined for the port of delivery, is diverted to an intermediate country where it is off-loaded and sold as "surplus." If the shipper is the perpetrator of this swindle, he collects the proceeds of the second deal and is thus paid twice for the same goods. If the shipper is honest then the guilty party may be the ship owner, the charterer or the ship's master. They may all be partners in crime.

To conceal the fraud, the ship may cease to exist. It may end up on the sea bed or continue under a new name and a new flag. One reason why this type of crime continues unabated is that many countries insist on their traders buying shipping insurance locally, so that the loss is borne by the victim country and not by the international maritime insurance market. The victim country, which thus pays twice over (for the goods and then the insurance loss) rarely possesses the machinery for investigating and bringing to justice this sophisticated form of fraud, which makes life easier for the criminal.

A typical example is the story of the tomato paste. The ship involved was the *M.V. Mariner* (1,338 gross tonnes) registered at Piraeus and owned by Ioannis Papaioannou and Vasilios Alexandros Papaioannou of Athens. On November 1, 1977, she was chartered by Asteris S.A., also of Athens, to deliver cans of tomato paste to Tripoli, Libya. The shipment was divided into two cargoes of 100,000 cartons containing filled cans plus 46 bundles (2,000 pieces) of empty cartons weighing 2,061 tonnes and 10,000 cartons of filled cans plus five bundles (200 pieces) of empty cartons weighing 206 tonnes. The total value was 1,300,200 U.S. dollars, insurance being placed with the Libya Insurance Company. The consignee was the National Supply Corporation of Tripoli.

The *Mariner* started loading at Katakolon, Greece, on November 3 and completed on November 11, the bills of lading being signed by the master, Captain Constantin Gritzalis. Minor repairs delayed the ship's departure until November 28, during which time she was sold to Frygia Compania Naviera S.A. of Panama, the new owners agreeing to honour the charter obligation.

On November 29, the day after sailing, Captain Gritzalis radioed his estimated time of arrival at Tripoli as December 1. However, on December 3 reports started to spread that some canned tomato paste, similar to that loaded onto the *Mariner*, was on offer through local brokers at Beirut. The master extended his E.T.A. to December 3 and then to December 5, and—according to reports that started to circulate in Athens—had signalled his familly that he was making for Beirut. This fitted in with other reports that the new owners had signalled him via Radio Cyprus that he was to put into Beirut because of congestion at Tripoli.

The shippers, Asteris S.A. attempted to contact the new owners at an address they had been given in Cyprus, but it proved to be false. Becoming somewhat alarmed, they asked the district attorney in Athens to ask Interpol to locate the ship, alerted various Greek Government departments and security services as well as Lloyd's Intelligence Service. Inquiries were hampered by reports coming in that *Mariner* had changed her name not once, but several times. She became *Arine 1, Aloha* and *Marina K*. In mid-January Lloyd's agent at Bissau, West Africa, reported the arrival of *Tarina T,* which discharged 110,000 cartons of tomato paste.

With the non-arrival of the shipment at Tripoli, Asteris's alarm increased and in mid-March a loss investigator from London arrived at Bissau. Lloyd's agent, A. Sotto Maior Limitada, showed him quantities of cartons of tomato paste in the port area. They bore the name of Asteris and the cans were printed with the brand name "Sandy," which corresponded with the missing shipment. The Bissau Customs Department was asked to block movements of the paste until its legal ownership was established. Inquiries showed that 10,000 cartons had been sold locally, the importer being named as Moukarim N. Camal of a firm named Magus. This man explained that he was merely an agent and that as he operated on behalf of some 2,000 principals, he was not able immediately to produce the name of the company he represented in this particular case. Later, he denied any involvement in the transaction.

This denial was made by telephone to the office of the Lloyd's agent. The following day, March 17, 1978, a representative of the Governor of Guinea Bissau's Central Bank arrived at the agent's office and started to question the loss investigator about this telephone conversation. Neither the agent nor the investigator had mentioned this, which suggested that either Moukarim had or the line had been tapped. The visitor revealed that Moukarim had originally applied for permission to land 2,200 tonnes of tomato paste for storage and eventual disposal, either by re-exporting or placing it on the local market.

Just when it appeared that the investigator from London was making headway with his inquiries, the local authorities started to make things difficult. The Port Office said that it kept no records of trans-shipment cargo and was unable to say how much had been landed from *Tarina T,* how much remained and how much had been re-exported. However, if permission had been sought and granted to land 2,200 tonnes, some form of official control on quantities would have been made.

Returning empty handed from the Port Office, the investigator found that the director general of Customs had visited Lloyd's agent and demanded to see the Briton's official credentials. He also learned that a commission to inquire into the tomato paste had been set up and asked permission to appear before it. This was initially granted but later withdrawn. He then tried to seek legal representation but was told that as Guinea Bissau was without civil or commercial law, lawyers could only be appointed by the Government and then only in criminal proceedings.

On March 21 a Miss Steflan was appointed by the Ministry of Justice as a public advocate to determine if there had been any criminal action. She gave news that neither she nor the United Kingdom investigator would be allowed to address the commission. She also made it clear that the Customs would not reply to questions from the Ministry of Justice regarding the tomato paste. Any attempts to seize or even prevent the movement of the cargo would result in heavy penalties. However, she did later reveal that cartons of tomato paste were being loaded onto a ship named *Gale* for an undisclosed destination. This was because the Commission, which had completed its inquiries, had decided that the cargo could be re-exported. It had reached this conclusion after studying papers which Moukarim had been permitted to place before it, in the absence of any papers from the loss investigator that gave proof that the goods were destined for Libya.

Such documents existed and had been offered to Miss Steflan who had declined to take them, saying that they would be called for later. The case was closed. Moukarim had been able to have his say, and the investigator had not. However, Lloyd's agent was able to obtain some figures. Ten thousand cartons had been sold to two local firms, 75,000 cartons were being loaded onto the *Gale* and another 25,000 cartons were available for local disposal. This accounted for the 110,000 which had formed the original consignment loaded in Greece for Libya.

But where was the Panama-registered *Gale* going to? Her destination was rumoured to be Dubai, but it was thought that Conakry, further along the West African coast, was a more likely port.

To obtain a visa for the Republic of Guinea involved a flight to Paris but this achieved, the investigator reached Conakry on April 14, 1978. There he found a ship in all appearances similar to the *Gale* but now called *Daler* busily discharging cartons of tomato paste. Conakry provided one advantage over Bissau: a Libyan chargé d'affaires, Abdul Gassim.

He accompanied the man from the United Kingdom to the Ministère du Domaine des Echanges where, in front of senior officials, documents were produced providing that the cargo now being unloaded from the *Daler* was the property of the Libyans. The Guinea authorities asked for further documentary details of the shipment as well as a letter requesting that the cargo be held in the customs area until its future was decided.

Strangely, Lloyd's agents, Paterson Zochonia Guinee S.A., said that they had received no request from Lloyd's Intelligence to look out for the *Gale* and her cargo. The agents and the port captain tried without success to contact the ship's master but one of the crew—an Egyptian—complained about the lack of food and money on board, volunteering the information that the ship had changed her name four times in three months, while her flag had been switched from Greek to Panamanian. He could not recall the first name but the others were *Melanie*, *Daler* and *Gale*. The present master, he said, had joined at Bissau.

Port records showed that she had berthed on March 29, 1978, to discharge 1,530 tonnes of tomato paste, said to be from Las Palmas for the Panama Attaché. Later, Abdul Gassim was able to extract an admission from the captain that the goods had been loaded at Bissau.

It was learned that a Swiss firm, Olivier International S.A. of Lausanne, had sold 75,000 cartons of tomato paste to Importex, the Guinea purchasing agency. Olivier's export manager, P.H. Kienberger, was in Conakry, and was soon found. He explained that his company had been offered the goods "at a very cheap price" by Etablissement Guimabi of Geneva. They had been told that the cargo was lying in Las Palmas and could be shipped to West Africa at the all-in price, with cash payable against documents through a bank. Olivier International thought the tomato paste to be a genuine sale, being in excess of requirement by the original purchaser.

The Swiss company had checked with a Swiss bank on the financial standing of the sellers and were advised that to the bank's knowledge, all was in order. Their purchasers demanded a sanitary certificate and one was issued at Las Palmas on March 6, together with other documents. These also appeared to be in order, although it was never made clear how a sanitary certificate could be issued in Las Palmas for a cargo being discharged from the *Tarina T* at Bissau. Olivier International, satisfied that all was above board, contacted Importex who immediately offered to buy the tomato paste at such a reasonable price.

Kienberger's first act now was to stop payment to Etablissement Guimabi, cancel the contract with Importex and suggest that the latter pay the Libyan insurance company the amount agreed by Olivier International—862,500 U.S. dollars. It would be feasible for the goods to be sent from Conakry to Libya, but the sensible answer seemed to be for them to be left in Conakry and for the Guinea Government to buy the cargo from the Libyans—the legal owner. It would save chartering a ship and in any case, tomato paste has a limited "shelf life."

This arrangement only solved part of the problem. There was still the 25,000 carton consignment in Bissau which might be recovered, but the 10,000 cartons already sold there were probably lost for ever.

Illegal Sinkings

The Salem

The loss of the supertanker *Salem* off the West Coast of Africa on January 17, 1980, might have passed off as a one-day news story in the world's press, for in the previous two years more than a hundred vessels had similarly foundered. Some had fallen victim to bad weather, others to faulty seamanship or maintenance, but many were believed to have been scuttled. Lloyd's of London maintain that in the course of a single year the costs of maritime crime to the world's insurance market rose to £110,000,000.

The dividing line between accepting a loss at sea as genuine and proving it to be fraudulent can be measured in months of exhausting, frustrating and costly enquiries involving the professional investigators, police forces, maritime officials and lawyers of several countries. It is sometimes cheaper for underwriters to settle a claim and close the files.

With *Salem* the insurance cover amounted to $24,000,000 for the hull and $60,200,000 for her cargo of crude oil. This was one reason—but not the only one—why the *Salem* story did not fade into oblivion. To start with, the ship's very dimensions were enough to arouse unusual interest. If this was scuttling, then it was king-sized. A ship more than three football fields in length, more than 70 feet longer than the Queen Elizabeth II cannot lose itself beneath the ocean without causing speculation. To add to it all, the reports themselves were puzzling.

It was said that although the *Salem* took hours to sink following a series of explosions, distress signals were not transmitted until another ship came into sight, and that while some of the rescued crew carried packed suitcases and freshly cut sandwiches, for quite inexplicable reasons there was no time for the ship's log to be saved.

The *Salem* was allegedly carrying 193,000 tons of crude oil, yet the oil slick left floating on the surface, although stretching for several miles, was far too modest for such an amount. Then came rumour of a secret stop en route at Durban and oil being clandestinely pumped ashore—at first vociferously denied by the South African government, only later to be admitted somewhat grudgingly as fact.

The *Salem* continued to develop into a maritime saga of mystery and intrigue, setting in motion a mass of speculation concerning piracy, sanctions busting and documentary fraud. It took unexpected twists such as the sudden decision by Master Sergeant Samuel Doe, fresh from his coup d'état in Liberia, to set free two prime suspects who had been detained in connection with the affair by his country's previous administration.

In shipping and marine insurance, the act of illegally selling off cargo before its intended destination is reached and deliberately scuttling the ship to claim insurance on both goes under the popular name of rust-bucket fraud, mainly because the ships involved are usually rust-ridden and barely seaworthy.

The *Salem* was not in this class. She was built in 1969 in Kockums' shipyard at Malmö, Sweden, for her owners, Salenrederierna AB of

Stockholm, and was named *Sea Sovereign*. She was heralded as the most advanced ship of the Swedish merchant fleet—1,037 feet in length, 160 in breadth and 80 feet deep, of 92,228 gross tons and 215,000 cwt, powered by a steam turbine developing 32,000 shaft horespower to a single propeller, and capable when carrying more than 200,000 tons of cargo oil of a speed of 16.1 knots. For this she needed 141 tons of bunker oil every 24 hours. She was equipped with four steam-driven main cargo pumps, an electrically driven bilge pump and two general service pumps which could take suction from the engine room bilges.

Early in the seventies she was sold to the Liberian registered Pimmerton Shipping company and her name changed to *South Sun*. Her last run for this company, in the last months of 1979, was from Chile to Dubai, where she was laid up awaiting a buyer. On several occasions she had called at South Africa, possibly for bunkers, possibly to deliver oil.

During 1979 an oil broking company was established in Pretoria (with an office in Johannesburg) called Haven International. With the loss of Iranian supplies and faced with an embargo by Arab producers, South Africa was increasingly being forced to buy oil on the spot market. The Arab embargo was imposed not because of the republic's domestic racial policy but because her wealthy Jewish population was the largest financial contributor after the United States, to Israel.

One man who appeared in Johannesburg, anxious to do business, was Fred Soudan. Lebanese-born but a naturalised American (with a home in Missouri City, Texas) he was 31, an ex-insurance salesman with a desire to get into oil shipping. His main need was capital in order to buy a tanker and the crude to be transported in it. Haven International was in a position to introduce him to local financial sources.

Soudan then approached a Greek shipbroking company, Northern Ships, run by Andrew Triandafilou and John Avgerinos, explaining his need for a tanker. Before they could find one, Soudan heard of *South Sun* and arranged to purchase her from Pimmerton for 11,500,000 U.S. dollars. He later changed her name to *Salem*. Soudan explained his new found wealth to a legacy from his father, but it was later believed that the money for the deal came from a South African bank.

Soudan was in need of a company to own his purchase and here Triandafilou and Avgerinos were in a position to help. For some years they had owned Oxford Shipping, a Liberian-registered company. They agreed to dispose of it to Soudan, payment being subject to a special agreement. The date of this transaction was November 27, 1979, and of the *South Sun* purchase November 29. Oxford Shipping had no trouble in finding business. *Salem* was immediately chartered bareboat to another Liberian concern, Shipomex, through a Rotterdam broker named Anton Reidel. Bareboat means that the owner has no responsibility for the crew or activities of the ship.

Shipomex was a newly created company with offices in Switzerland. Its director was a man known to most people connected with the *Salem* affair as Bert Stein. Stein arranged for *Salem* to go to Kuwait and load 193,000 tons of crude oil on behalf of the Italian trading company Pontoil and transport it to Genoa. Pontoil got hold of Stein through their London shipbrokers who contacted the Greek ship-brokers, Genpe. Genpe in turn were approached by a Captain Mytakis of Mitnizafir Navigation Company of Piraeus with the news that the *Salem* (at that time still called *South Sun*) was available for a charter and that he was acting for Shipomex. The deal was completed on November 29, the same day as the *South Sun* was sold to Soudan. Captain Mytakis had already been asked by Stein to find a crew for the supertanker and had done so.

The master he had selected was Captain Dimitrios Georgoulis, who proved to be a man with an interesting past. Born in Greece in 1937, he had decided to make the sea his career and apart from a two-year spell (1969-70) when he lived with his brother in America, he had worked his way up to master of several ships. Yet he had never held a Liberian or Greek licence of any type, possessing only a chief mate's licence from the Republic of Panama.

The chief engineer, Antonios Kalomiropoulos, also Greek born (1947), had studied at a marine engineering school in Athens and held licences as chief engineer from both Greece and Liberia. Later both men claimed that they had been recruited as the result of an advertisement by Captain Mytakis and while in his office had met Stein who they understood represented the owners of the ship on which they would work. The owners, they were told, were still without an actual ship but were interested in the *Paola*, a steam tanker of about 210,000 cwt, then at Gibraltar. Georgoulis was engaged as master at 3,000 dollars a month and the other man as chief engineer at 3,500 dollars a month.

They were both sent to Gibraltar to inspect the *Paola* and sailed in her to Malta where a crew was sent to join them. However, the *Paola* deal collapsed and the men waited until they were instructed to fly to Dar es Salaam to wait for the *South Sun*, which was being purchased instead. It was now mid-November.

The ship did not materialise at the Tanzanean port and they were instructed to go to Dubai, where they found her waiting in ballast. On November 27 the new crew of 15 Greeks and 10 Tunisians took over from the ship's original 42 Chinese. On December 3 the name of *Salem* was adopted.

Only after the *Salem*'s sinking was Georgoulis's name to be linked with other mysterious maritime dramas. He was said to be under investigation for alleged fraud in connection with the loss in May 1979 of the freighter *Alexandros K* while on her way from Bulgaria to Egypt with a 1,160,000 dollars cargo of steel bars. Like the *Salem,* she foundered, by which time the steel had been landed in the Lebanon, for which operation her name was changed to *Leila* .

The owners of the Liberian-registered *Alexandros K* were also owners of the 2,633 ton cargo ship *Brilliant* which sank off Sicily in 1975 while supposedly carrying valuable scrap metal. As with the *Salem*, it was alleged that hours passed before distress signals were transmitted and then only when help was close at hand. Both ships—*Salem* and *Brilliant*—had the same radio operator. Lloyd's of London faced a claim for 600,000 dollars for the *Brilliant*'s loss.

After the *Salem* sinking it transpired that Georgoulis had joined the ship in defiance of a police order prohibiting him from leaving Greece because of the *Alexandros K* affair. He slipped out using an American passport in the name of Jimmy Georgoulis.

He took over the *South Sun* and sailed her to Mina Al Ahmadi, Kuwait, where she took on the 193,000 tons of crude. She sailed for Italy on December 10. Four days later the oil changed hands. Pontoil sold the entire shipment to Shell International for 56,000,000 dollars (about £25,000,000). Mid-voyage deals are quite common in the spot oil market.

On December 27 the supertanker dropped anchor off Durban harbour, but she was no longer called the *Salem*. The crew had changed her name to *Lema*. She then pumped 173,000 tons of her cargo into an oil terminal point one and a half miles off shore. Afterwards she took on seawater to replace the missing oil, thereby creating the appearance that she was still laden with her original cargo. This was in accordance with the special agreement already mentioned covering the purchase of Oxford Shipping. Soudan had agreed to pay the two Greeks, Triandafilou and Avgerinos, 300,000 dollars brokerage fees on or about December 27, 1979,

"upon the arrival of the vessel *South Sun* off Durban, South Africa (closing date) or any other discharge port ... this agreement is exclusively contingent upon and subject to the lifting of the cargo of crude oil by the vessel South Sun and the arrival of the vessel at Durban, South Africa, and the commencement of the discharge. In the event that the said contingency does not occur, the purchaser shall then pay the sellers the amount of twenty-five thousand dollars ($25,000.00) in consideration of the purchase of the said stock...."

The agreement was dated November 27, but was signed by Soudan on December 8 and by the two Greeks on December 10.

While the crew worked on the *Salem*, now *Lema,* Captain Georgoulis went ashore to meet Haven International's representatives at a hotel. Haven International had no idea that the tanker was to be scuttled. In fact, they were expecting further shipments of crude in the months ahead.

Shortly before the *Salem*'s visit, Anton Reidel flew into Johannesburg with documents proving the availability of the oil and to collect the money. Information about the actual amount he received was obscured by the South African ban on publicity of its oil transactions (the country's Oil Procurement Act can impose fines of £6,500 and five years in prison against people found guilty of divulging details of oil shipments and financial transactions). Early in January an event took place that brought unwelcome publicity to the whole *Salem* affair. While attempting to complete the deal, Soudan discovered that Triandafilou and Avgerinos, who possibly doubted to his ability to find the money, were trying to sell Oxford Shipping and with it the tanker, to Reidel.

When the original deal covering the sale of Oxford Shipping was drawn up, it was agreed that Triandafilou and Avgerinos would elect Soudan as President and Director and his wife Anna Maria Soudan as Secretary and Director and then to resign themselves from the board. It was further provided that pending the arrival in Durban of a cargo of crude oil certain documents, corporate books and seal were to be held by lawyers representing the two Greeks.

On December 24, a letter headed Oxford Shipping Company Inc. was delivered to the Deputy Commissioner of Maritime Affairs of Liberia in New York, stating that at a special meeting of shareholders on that day, Fred Soudan was removed from his post as President/Director and Anna Maria Soudan from her position as Secretary/Director, their places being taken by the two Greeks. It was signed by Triandafilou.

Soudan filed a suit in New York on January 4 against the Greeks alleging violation of agreement and seeking to prevent them transferring the stock to Anton Reidel. It was then that the special agreement concerning the South African operation was mentioned. On January 14 the Admiralty Counsel of the Bureau of Maritime Affairs was advised that the dispute had been settled in Soudan's favour and that a stipulation to this effect would be submitted the next day to the New York Supreme Court.

The next day after that, at approximately 0355 hours on January 16, according to crew members, the fire alarm sounded on board *Salem* (now no longer called the *Lema*), to be followed by a muffled explosion. The tanker's position was 12° 38′ north, 18° 34′ west and she was off the coast of Senegal.

She had by then covered 8,634 nautical miles from Mina Al

Ahmadi. At an average speed of 12 knots this should have taken 30 days, or ony 27 if she had been doing 13 knots, as some of the crew maintained. As it was she had taken 38 days, the delay being later blamed on repairs to a port boiler. But at the subsequent questioning in Liberia, some crew members said that this slowed the vessel down for only eight days while others said it lasted 15 days.

The explosion on the morning of the 16th was forward of the deck house and in the area of the pump room. In the early morning twilight smoke could be seen coming from the bows. The engine room crew stopped the engines and the engine room itself started to take water. The pumps were switched on. Georgoulis, it seems, did not wait to assess the damage but ordered the crew to the two lifeboats. He later claimed that he told the radio operator to send out an SOS on the temporary radio transmitter aboard one of the lifeboats, giving their position as 120 miles south west of Dakar. Later investigations failed to produce any evidence that these signals were actually transmitted, let alone heard by any ship or shore station.

According to the crew, the *Salem* was abandoned at 0430 on January 16. Accounts vary, but claims were made that a second explosion occurred about 0800, and a much louder one at 0400 on January 17, causing the navigation lights to go out. At about 1030 the *British Trident* was passing and radio signals were heard.

The two lifeboats were reached 30 minutes later. It was about this time that the *Salem* rolled over to starboard and sank stern first.

At the later investigation Georgoulis's reason for not probing the cause of the explosion was that he feared further ones could endanger life. The chief engineer gave a similar reason for not investigating the source of the water in the engine room.

The *British Trident* took the crew to Dakar where most of them were flown back to Greece. Here they were interviewed by Captain A. I. Tzamtziz, a marine safety officer for the Republic of Liberia. Their stories varied. Some claimed that in addition to smoke they saw fire aboard. Yet Captain David Bruce, in charge of the Liberian Regional Marine Safety Office in London, was told by the crew of the *British Trident* that they saw no signs of smoke or fire when they reached the *Salem*. Some of the *Salem*'s crew claimed that there were a series of explosions throughout the 16th, yet the British ship's men said they saw no signs of structural damage to the *Salem*.

In Liberia, the *Salem*'s master and engineer denied reports that they had put into Durban. While they were doing so Detective Chief Superintendent Peter Griggs and Detective Inspector Reginald Golding of Scotland Yard's fraud squad were making enquiries in South Africa. They discovered Georgoulis's signature in the register of Durban's Royal Hotel and on delivery receipts of supplies to the *Lema*.

They traced telephone calls he had made to Greece and Switzerland, one being to Mytakis. They found that he had stayed ashore with the wife of the ship's electrician and arranged for her to fly home from Durban to Greece. They also found that a crew member—a Tunisian—had been taken ill and brought ashore for treatment.

They also collected a statement given by a Tunisian crew member to lawyers for London underwriters that the *Salem* had been scuttled by the removal of certain plates and manholes.

The *British Trident*'s officers made an inventory of property found in the two *Salem* lifeboats. There came to 151 items not normally forming part of lifeboat equipment, ranging from hacksaws to navigational equipment usually found on a ship's bridge. Other incriminating evidence was a record of radio telephone calls made from a vessel identified as the *Lema* but using call letters belonging to the *Salem*. Not least damaging was the admission on February 2 by South Africa's Minister for Internal Industry, Trade and Commerce, Dr. Schalk van der Merwe that the ship had delivered oil to his country.

It soon emerged that the oil had been purchased on behalf of Sasol, the petrol-from-coal corporation. Because it does not produce sufficient petrol to meet South Africa's needs, crude oil has still to be imported and Sasol itself owns a conventional refinery in partnership with French and Iranian oil interests. Natref, as it is called, generally concentrates on aviation and other special fuels. It was also suggested that some of the shipment from the *Salem* was bound for Rhodesia.

For the South African government it was one thing to participate in sanctions busting. It was quite another to be connected with a massive fraud.

Although the Liberian inquiry recommended that Georgoulis and Kalomiropoulos be held in connection with the *Salem* affair, they were freed by that country's new leader.

On 4th August 1980, warrants were issued at the Guildhall Magistrates Court in the City of London for the arrest of Frederick Ed Soudan, believed to reside at Houston, Texas; Anton Reidel (Senior) believed to live in Holland; Johannes Locks also known as Bert Stein, believed to reside in Frankfurt, West Germany; and Dimitrious Georgoulis, believed to reside in Greece.

1. That they on divers days between 1st September 1979 and 18th April 1980 conspired together and with the Oxford Shipping Company Incorporated of Monrovia and with other persons to defraud Lowndes Lambert Group and divers companies and persons in London, Liverpool and Norway who undertook to insure the hull and machinery of the vessel "Salem" formerly "South Sun" for the sum of U.S. $24 million in respect of marine

and other risks by falsely and dishonestly pretending that the said vessel had foundered and been lost as a result of accident whereas in truth she was intended to be and was deliberately scuttled. Against the peace.

2. For that they the said Frederick Ed Soudan, Anton Reidel, Johannes Locks and Dimitrious Georgoulis on divers days between 1st September 1979 and 18th January 1980 conspired together and with the Oxford Shipping Company of Monrovia, Shipomex S.A., Beets Trading Ag, American Polomax International Incorporated and with other persons to defraud such persons in the U.K. as might be induced to charter the vessel "Salem" formerly "South Sun" and to purchase a cargo of oil to be loaded onto the said vessel by falsely and dishonestly pretending that the vessel would sail for the benefit of the charterers and would deliver the said cargo of oil in accordance with the instructions of the charterers whereas in truth the conspirators had undertaken to and did in fact sail the vessel to a port of their own choosing and did there deliver the cargo of oil for a sum in excess of $44 million U.S. to South African purchasers in South Africa. Against the peace.

It may be that, one day, those named in the arrest warrants may become available for trial in England. However, one cannot doubt that the warrants are a purely cosmetic device by the British authorities to show that they are alive to the problem and can be seen to be doing something. If substantive offences have been committed, they must necessarily have been committed outside United Kingdom jurisdiction by reason of the known facts. The warrants are drawn upon the basis of a conspiracy to defraud United Kingdom insurance interests, a crime for which there can be no extradition from those countries where the alleged offenders are.

6 Flags of Convenience

Whenever one reads the proceedings of an international conference on maritime crime, the phrase "flags of convenience" is bound to come up in discussion often with overtones of the most sinister kind. There will always be at least one speaker prepared to attribute many of the problems to ships sailing under such "flags," suggesting that if the flag of convenience were to be abolished, so too would crime associated with carriage of goods by sea. Some measure of support for this view can be gained from a valuable analysis prepared by a leading cargo underwriter, of 52 cases of non-delivery or mis-delivery of cargo.[1]

"An analysis of the 52 cases involved shows an interesting situation:

A. *By flag*

Cyprus	11 cases
Greece	24 cases
Liberia	2 cases
Panama	15 cases

B. *By age*

0—15 years	9 cases
15—20 years	14 cases
21—25 years	17 cases
26—30 years	10 cases
31—35 years	2 cases

C. *By gross registered tonnage*

501—2,500	5 cases
2,501—5,000	10 cases
5,001—7,500	15 cases
7,501—10,000	16 cases
10,000 and over	6 cases

Nearly all the cases where Panama flag vessels were concerned are in respect of ownerships registered in the Far East. None of the reported cases can be attributed to vessels complying with the new 'regular pattern of trading' wording in the terms of the new Classification Clause or the so-called 'Liner' trading definition of the previous clause."

---

[1] The reader may be interested in comparing these figures with those at (p.2). Bearing in mind that the basis upon which they were compiled is different.

Other interesting features of this particular analysis were that many of the vessels involved were chartered on the occasion about which complaint was made; that the majority were in single vessel ownership although sometimes in common management, and that more than a few changed names just before the event or shortly afterwards. These facts were reported to the Institute of Chartered Shipbrokers first seminar on maritime fraud in a paper written and presented by Mr. A. Perry of the Salvage Association. He concluded his address by quoting a letter from a firm of shippers to a shipping and forwarding agent.

"Re: Shipment of our orders
We have the impression that a number of malafide ship's owners and or charterers try again to make our life and that of other shippers difficult. Vessels on which our cargo sail are diverted to some odd ports and only after paying the freight (or part of it) once more it might be possible that the goods arrive at destination. Sometimes, however, the goods have already been sold by the master of the vessel to recover salaries of the crew bunker and port charges, etc. In order to try to avoid such misevents in future we request you:

    (1) Before booking our cargo on Greek, Cypriot, Liberian, Panamese or Taiwanese flag vessels, please ask our approval, indicating (a) vessel's name and age; (b) vessel's owner; (c) whether vessel has been chartered and if affirmative the name and address of this company.

    (2) To find out whether the line, with which you anticipate to ship, is a reliable one.

On basis of information gathered by our company we have made a 'black list' of vessels of malafide owners. At the same time we wish to add however, that this list is not complete and moreover you know that the names of vessels (and owners) are changed as easy as the direction of the wind."

To discover what a flag of convenience is, one must look at ship registration as a whole and a useful starting point is to scan, quite briefly, the requirements for registration in the United Kingdom. These requirements are stated in the principle statute, the Merchant Shipping Act 1894. Those sections of interest in this particular study form only a tiny part of the whole and may be précised as follows:

Section 1: Qualifications for owning a British ship

A ship shall not be deemed a British ship unless wholly owned by: (a) British subjects, or (b) bodies corporate established under and subject to the laws of H.M. Dominions or having their principal place of business in those dominions.

Section 2: Obligation to register British ships

  (1) Every British shop shall, unless exempted from registry, be registered under this Act.
  (2) If a ship required by this Act to be registered is not registered under this Act she shall not be registered as a British ship.

Section 4: Registrars of British ships

This section provides that registration must take place with the Chief Officer of Customs at a British port of the owner's chosing.

Section 47: Rules as to name of ship

This section makes it an offence for a master or owner to change a ship's name without prior written consent from the relevant department.

There is no statutory penalty for failure to register a British ship in accordance with section 2, however, the omission results in forfeiture of the protection available and due to British ships whilst away from their home ports. This protection stems from the fact that a ship is considered a part of the country under whose flag it sails. The unlawful detention of a British ship and improper conduct towards its crew would be a matter of concern for H.M. Government and one can visualise circumstances in which considerable diplomatic pressure might be brought to bear on a power giving such offence. Lesser incidents have brought nations into sabre-rattling confrontation where the sovereignty of one has been challenged through the medium of its shipping.

A clear definition of a flag of convenience state may be somewhat difficult when considered in a wide economic and social context, because the term can be applied to some when used in one sense and others when used differently. A useful definition appeared in the Rochdale report (Committee of Inquiry into Shipping, Cmnd. 4337, HMSO).

  (1) The country of registry allows ownership and/or control of its merchant vessels by non-citizens.
  (2) Access to the register is easy. A ship may usually be registered at a Consul's office abroad. Equally important, transfer from the registry at the owner's option is not restricted.
  (3) Taxes on the income from the ships are not levied locally or are low. A registry fee and an annual fee, based on tonnage,

are normally the only charges made. A guarantee or acceptable understanding regarding future freedom from taxation may also be given.

(4) The country of registration is a small power with no national requirement under any foreseeable circumstances for all the shipping registered, but receipts from very small charges on a large tonnage may produce a substantial effect on its national income and balance of payments.

(5) Manning of ships by non-nationals is freely permitted.

(6) The country of registry has neither the power nor the administrative machinery effectively to impose any government or international regulations; nor has the country the wish to control the companies themselves.

Two further definitions appear in the EEC Shipping Policy Opinion:

"There are two equivalent definitions of 'flag of convenience':

A flag of convenience can be defined as a flag of any country allowing the registration of foreign owned and foreign controlled vessels under conditions which, for whatever reasons, are convenient and opportune for the persons who are registering the vessels. (Boczek, B.A., "Flags of Convenience," Cambridge, Mass., 1962, page 2)

A flag of convenience can be defined as the flag of such countries whose law allows—and indeed make it easy—for ships owned by foreign nationals or companies to fly those flags in contrast to the practice in the maritime countries where the right to fly the national flag is subject to stringent conditions and involves far-reaching obligations. (Maritime Transport Committee of the OECD: Study of the expansion of the flags of convenience and of various aspects thereof, quoted in Boczek, page 3)"

The Opinion records 17 states as having flags of convenience or quasi flags of convenience, of which the first five are the most certain and significant:

1. Liberia	10. Lebanon
2. Panama	11. Seychelles
3. Singapore	12. Cayman Isles
4. Cyprus	13. Maldive Isle
5. Somalia	14. Netherland Antilles
6. Bermuda	15. Malta
7. Bahamas	16. Oman
8. Honduras	17. Hong Kong
9. Costa Rica	

The absence of Greece from the list may at first glance appear to be strange because Greek nationals are very well represented in shipping affairs and in particular in connection with flags of convenience. In fact, whilst conditions for registration under the Greek flag are considerably different from those of the United Kingdom, there are restrictions which prevent open registration and wholly free transfer. Greek influence can be illustrated by reference to *Table 9* of the *EEC Opinions:*

BENEFICIAL OWNERSHIP

"No reliable data is available on beneficial ownership of ships registered in FOC countries. The UNCTAD report TD/B/C4/168 was unsuccessful in establishing details of beneficial owners, since 48% remained unidentified. However, the new UNCTAD report presented to the Manila conference gives details of a study prepared by A & P Appledore International of London, which claims to have identified 98% of the total deadweight tonnage registered under flags of convenience. This shows that ownership is based primarily in the following countries:

United States	67,376 million tons deadweight
Greece	40,666 million tons deadweight
Hong Kong	33,304 million tons deadweight
Japan	18,105 million tons deadweight

A further statistic of some interest can be obtained from *Table 8* of the Opinion, with regard to total losses of ships in a period from 1971 until 1977. The mean loss ratio, expressed as a percentage of tonnage has been calculated for the EEC countries as 13 per cent. The same mean loss ratio for Liberia, Panama, Singapore and Cyprus is 1.25 per cent. When one knows that the EEC countries have 19 per cent. of the world's shipping tonnage registered within their systems, and the FOC countries have 27.7 per cent., the comparison of mean loss ratios takes on a great deal more significance. That difference is worth contemplating, too, in terms of the people who sail in merchant ships or those who trust their money and goods to those ships. Whilst it may be remotely possible to calculate losses in terms of wealth, directly attributable to the worse flag of convenience ships, no reliable notion can be gained of the cost in terms of death and injury to seamen resulting from employment in them.

By now it will have become obvious that there may be any numbers of reasons why some shipowners prefer to operate under a flag of convenience rather than their own national flag. Those reasons may include the obtaining of tax advantages, a flexibility of operation, or the desire to operate outside the restrictions applied by more conservative governments. Much of the world's tonnage and in particular tankers and bulk grain carriers, is operated under flags of convenience in a manner which, from safety and social considerations, is beyond reproach. Some is operated in a way that is quite disgraceful from any point of view. On the one hand there is a supertanker of the most modern design, fitted with every safety device available, plying its trade around the world on a regular route and crewed by first rate men working under ideal contracts of employment. On the other hand one can see rust-pocked hulls of ancient vintage, limping from port to port, dangerously deficient in equipment and crewed by ill-qualified and underpaid men with no security of employment. The first will be on a regular contract, carrying the property of a single shipper without difficulty or dispute between shipper and owner. The second will be offered as the means of transporting goods at cut-price freight, from anywhere to anywhere, with very obvious risks to anyone foolish enough to entrust its owners with a cargo.

There are a number of interests anxious to phase out or control flags of convenience for reasons of their own. This book is not the proper forum for a lengthy discussion on that particular aspect, it is nevertheless of some interest to have a broad outline of what is afoot. First, but not necessarily the most important or influential is the ITF (International Transport Workers Federation). This organisation has for its aims the welfare of seamen on whatever ships they sail. These aims are set out in a booklet directed to potential recruits:

> "*How the ITF protects seafarers*
> The main task is clearly that of protecting the seafarers themselves. That can only be done by making sure, (a) that all crews are covered by proper trade union agreements safeguarding their wages and working conditions and (b) that those agreements are fully implemented by the owners wherever their ships may be trading."

One method of achieving this aim has been the appointment of inspectors in countries all around the world and, from the ITF's literature one gets the impression that considerable impact has been and is being made.

Many nations are themselves interested in repatriating ships sailing under a flag of convenience which they claim should properly be sailing under the national flag. There may seem to be an element of justice in this view when, by employing his assets in such a way, a citizen is depriving his own government of potential income derived from registration fees and tonnage taxes to the benefit of some "flag" state, coupled often with the loss to tax havens of profits which might have been subject to other forms of taxation. The EEC, too, is edging towards a policy of phasing out flags of convenience within the Community for both political and economic reasons; politically, in the belief that Community members should have the opportunity, in time of emergency, to exercise a degree of control over ships owned by Community citizens; economically because it is felt that member states are entitled to a proper share of taxable profits. Predictably, there is considerable opposition to any suggestion of phasing out and it hardly needs saying that the opposition comes from owners and operators who find the flag of convenience "convenient and opportune."

The term "flag of convenience" has existed for very many years and, imprecise as it is, has been used throughout this chapter. Readers who are unfamiliar with the topic might wish to know, however, that there are other terms used, often synonymously and with a similar lack of accuracy. Of these the terms "cheap flag" and "tax haven flag" are the only ones of importance. Terms such as "phoney flags" and "runaway flags" have an emotive quality about them which suggests that their user is somewhat less than objective without adding anything to the discussion. The "Opinion" offers the following definitions:

(1) *Cheap flags* Cheap flags are a special form of flags of convenience. A flag of convenience is acquired through expatriation or flag transfer "for whatever reason."

If, however, the term "cheap flag" or "cheap flag country" is to be appropriate, then the narrower criteria developed in the Rochdale Report (and adopted by the OECD) must be satisfied. These criteria will be found set out at page 63.

(2) *Tax haven countries/flags* Tax haven countries can be distinguished from flag of convenience countries and "cheap flag" countries. Shipping companies domiciled in tax haven countries do of course enjoy considerable tax advantages. But as regards crews, safety and certificates of competence, the tax haven countries have requirements similar to those of the traditional seafaring nations.

Whether a flag is regarded as a flag of convenience, a "cheap flag" or a tax haven flag can vary considerably over a period of time, depending upon the conditions offered by the country in question. For example, in 1970 Morocco, San Marino, Haiti, Malta and Sierra Leone were still regarded as "cheap flag" countries, whereas only Bermuda, the Bahamas, Gibraltar and the Netherland Antilles were classed as tax haven countries by the OECD. For Sweden the German flag even for a certain time counted as a flag of convenience (although not as a "cheap flag") since operating costs under German regulations were found to be lower than under the Swedish flag.

Consequently all the concepts are of a relative nature, and the classification of a country/flag is liable to vary over a period of time.

Whatever may be the advantages or disadvantages attaching to a system of registration in which ships may be operated under the flag of state to which owners have no genuine link, there can be little doubt of a co-relation between *some* flags of convenience vessels and *some* maritime crime. A study of the examples contained within this volume will be the best corroboration of that particular assertion.

7 International Organisations

In an industry such as shipping, it is inevitable that there will be a number of associations formed to protect various interests. Some will be formed to protect the rights of shippers, some for the enhancement of crew's conditions; others for the benefit of shipowners; international ones whose base is political and perhaps others whose objects are for the interchange of information or largely social. Not all of these associations, authorities groups, conferences or whatever they may be called hold much interest for those wishing to know something about maritime crime, but many of them have a connection, sometimes marginal, which makes it advisable to have a passing knowledge of their position in the scheme of things. What will become obvious as one reviews these bodies is that there is no single organisation whose *raison d'être* is to control, investigate or prevent marine fraud or, indeed, any other form of marine and airborne crime. As near as one can get to an internationally concerned body is the International Association of Airport and Seaport Police (IAASP) whose influence is rising rapidly despite the fact that it is both unofficial and voluntary. It is unofficial in that it does not have the financial backing of any national government; voluntary in the sense that its members join because they are interested in its objects and recognise its value to them in whatever capacity they work.

The EEC and United Nations, through the medium of agencies have some part to play in the control of crime and there are a number of commercial institutions such as Lloyds whose connection is through being regular victims of crime. There follows an outline of some of those organisations whose constitution and objects are of interest to the student of maritime crime but their importance is not necessarily related to the amount of space they have been allotted. It may seem that august bodies have been treated very lightly indeed, whilst relatively lightweight organisations have been given a more comprehensive treatment. It is to be hoped the reasons for this approach will be justified in the reading.

Police Organisations

The IAASP

This association has its origins in Boston, Massachusetts, and was formed as a central organisation through which information and co-operation between various North American and Canadian law agencies could develop. In a relatively short time, the original members discovered that there was a worldwide interest in controlling crime associated with ports and so in 1974, the association went truly international and was launched under its present title.

The association then wrote its constitution and into it put the following objectives:

(1) To prevent and detect criminal activity affecting the international shipment of cargo.

(2) To study and recommend methods and uniform practices for establishing safeguards against loss of international cargo.

(3) To encourage and develop the exchange of information and material among law enforcement agencies concerned with criminal activities in the seaports and airports.

(4) To encourage co-operation between the segments of the international trade community for the development of improved security measures for international cargo.

The constitution of the association allows for membership in two classes:

(1) Active members who are serving police officers and Government law enforcement officers, and

(2) Associate members who are those involved in other forms of port and cargo security activity such as insurance, carriers and trade associations concerned with the import or export of goods by sea and air.

At the association's inaugural meeting, Mr. Donald N. Cassidy, Director General of the National Harbours Board, Police and Security, Ottawa, said:

"Crime in the ports and harbours of the world present a serious problem to the society we live in. The problem is not unique to any one country. It does, however, damage the reputation of the ports and affects the economy of countries.

While there are all types of crime committed in harbours, the most prevalent is theft of cargo. No other crime committed against society has such international similarity in its modus operandi or universal effect on the world's economy as does cargo theft. It is one crime about which the port police forces of the world can communicate effectively, even through the barriers of language.

There is an obvious lack of co-ordinated effort on the part of police agencies with jurisdiction and responsibility in the ports of the world in the common task of fighting crime in these areas."

Perhaps a further quotation from an association speaker, Nae-Hyong Yoo, Superintendent General of the Korean National Police, addressing the Eighth Annual Conference, will help to illustrate the international flavour of its efforts.

> "It is needless to say at this point that international co-operation among law enforcement agencies of the world is a vital and decisive factor to the success of defeating international criminals. Exchange of information in the international police community is most essential.
>
> I know the IAASP has made great strides over the years in recognising the need for international co-operation. However, when the sciences of transportation and communication advance every day, such advancement benefits the criminals more rapidly than the law enforcement agencies."

A comment on these two extracts may be appropriate at this point, the first being that Mr. Cassidy's view of the most prevalent crime in harbours being theft of property, may well now have been overtaken by a broader view with the increase of containerisation, and that fraud of one kind or another accounts for some of the greatest losses. With regard to Mr. Nae-Hyong Yoo's address, one cannot help but feel that he was, whilst extolling the virtues of communication between members, unconsciously underlining the association's limitations. Those limitations, imposed purely by reason of international politics, should not be seen as inferring that the association is ineffective because nothing could be further from the truth. When one lives in a world where governments cannot co-operate effectively enough to prevent war, one cannot criticise those who voluntarily combine to control crime for being less than totally effective.

The IAASP carries a measure of authority in spite of its voluntary nature, because it has consultative status with the United Nations, is a corporate member of the International Association of Ports and Harbours and has strong links with the International Association of Chiefs of Police. There is also a very strong bond between the association and Interpol. It is non-governmental, non-sectarian, non-racial and non-political. It is governed by a board of directors who meet twice yearly, and who are drawn from the widest geographical spread possible. Annual meetings at which papers are presented and members make the vital person-to-person contact, are supplemented by circulated papers.

When one looks at the "active" member of the IAASP with regard to their individual status, one realises why the association's potential as an investigative body is limited and why its value as a preventive body is not as high as it might otherwise be. By reason of its constitution, active members of the association must be members of a law enforcement agency, a term covering a wide variety of responsibilities, by no means all financed by government funds. A leading agency, the Port of London Authority Police, has government support in that its officers receive training at Home Office Schools and are in daily contact and co-operation with the Metroplitan, Essex, and Kent Police forces. Its finance, however, is drawn from the Port of London Authority. The P.L.A. has no great reluctance to allow members of its police force to travel abroad when engaged upon matters within its jurisdiction and, finances such visits in instances where they are of only fringe benefit such as in connection with international crime. It does, too, provide facilities for collection and dissemination of information on maritime frauds reported from all over the world.

A glance down the 1978 list of directors is sufficient to demonstrate the variety of law enforcement agencies involved in the IAASP's activities. It includes officials from agencies as diverse as Keelung Harbour Police, Republic of China; Amsterdam Airport Police; Japanese National Police Force; Massachusetts State Police, U.S.A.; United States Customs Service and the Kelang Port Authority Police, Malaysia. These are, of course, only some representative authorities and it is fair to say that almost every major trading nation with the exception of the U.S.S.R. is represented either by group or individual membership. Associate directors were drawn from private investigators from Australia, London insurance executives and others.

Investigations in any form of crime may be carried out either by regularly appointed investigators such as officers of Criminal Investigation Departments, or, much less often by private investigators employed by commercial undertakings. C.I.D. officers of a United Kingdom police force operate within their own jurisdiction armed with powers granted by statute or common law, whereas private investigators have only those common law powers possessed by any other citizen. Common to both official and unofficial investigators is that, once beyond their own jurisdiction, their powers cease completely. Thus an investigator from England finding himself in, say, Marseilles, would have no power to do anything more to further his enquiry than simply ask questions which need never be answered, or seek aid from the French authorities. Collectively, a team from the IAASP drawn from half a dozen nations would be no better off because they would still have no jurisdiction whatever in a country to which none of them belong. It follows that there being no transferable jurisdiction, nor means by which an investigator can exercise power backed by legal sanction, the IAASP cannot therefore undertake investigative tasks for which its active members are very well qualified.

As though the difficulty of lack of jurisdiction was not enough, there is no fund of money available to finance an international investigation by members of the association. Any investigation carried out by an agent travelling and working away from his own country must necessarily be very expensive and to mount such investigations on a regular basis would require substantial expenditure. Responsibility for carrying out such regular investigations requires an efficient administration to back up those in the field. A suitable administrative base, if a single base would be adequate, must be sited at some centre of commerce with first grade communications again requiring considerable finance.

Having considered the association's objectives and its inherent limitations, one sees that it performs a vital function in the field of maritime crime but one that cannot be strained beyond a certain point. Where that point may be in the future is difficult to forecast because the energy of its governing body is considerable and the expertise of its members without parallel. It is highly improbable, however, that the association can develop into an integrated investigative body in the foreseeable future. Pehaps its true future may be in the mutual exchange of information and experience, and as a contact point for a differently constituted body whose personnel are free to travel wherever their enquiries take them. An interesting contrast can be made between the IAASP and Interpol, the one being a wholly voluntary organ and the other being firmly official.

Interpol

If any agencies in the world have ever been misunderstood, then the International Criminal Police Organisation must surely take first place among them. It is subject to a great deal of ill-informed comment, both by the news media and by writers searching for dramatic plots for film and television. Interpol does not allow for individual membership because only recognised police forces, sponsored by their national governments, may subscribe, if only because the organisation's finances are drawn from those governments. There is of course, no compulsion for any government to allow its police to become members and it follows that by no means all forces do so. However, it should not be thought that there is no co-operation between forces that belong and those that do not. On the contrary, when dictated by a nation's own interest, one sees examples of close contact and assistance between the most dissimilar forces. Some national police services are so different in their constitution, objects and degree of governmental control that comparisons between them are pointless. A force such as the Royal Canadian Police could not be compared in any way with the police of a repressive, one party state for example. One force will be a service devoted to the twin aims of preserving life and property under democratically enacted laws; the other a mere organ of state used to control the people. It may afford no cause for surprise to learn that the repressive administration seldom subscribes to Interpol.

Before one can understand where Interpol fits into the scheme of maritime crime, one needs to know what it is not: it is most certainly not a band of ace investigators who jet around the world arresting international criminals. Sad as it may be for the dramatist or the reporter having a scent of foreign connections in some local crime, Interpol is of a much less exciting character. It is, in essence, a channel of communication whose centre is in Paris. In the event of a police officer in an English police force requiring an enquiry in Naples, he will pass his request through the British representative at New Scotland Yard who will forward it to Paris for onward transmission to Rome and Naples. Perhaps rather more cumbersome and indirect than it might be, the system does have advantages where language difficulties exist and where methods of police operations are variable. For instance, those in the Paris headquarters would know from experience how much information the Neapolitan police need to conduct their enquiries effectively, as well as knowing what limitations may be placed upon them by local and national conditions. There is an information gathering function which forms such an important aspect of any police service, but with Interpol it is essentially international in character. An illustration of this particular activity in connection with a relatively minor form of crime, can be seen in an epidemic of pocket picking which troubled the police of many European cities a few years ago. By an international exchange of information between police forces through the Paris Bureau, it was soon discovered that the "dips" were a gang of experts from South America. With that information well distributed among member forces the gang were fairly quickly identified as they passed through airport immigration systems, and very rapidly caught and convicted.

In connection with maritime crime, Interpol performs the same function as with any other form of international dishonesty, namely that of acting as a channel of communication and a bureau for the exchange of information. That its function could be expanded to a considerable degree cannot be doubted and, as efforts to control this specialised form of dishonesty are accelerated, it may be that Interpol's involvement may become more apparent and even more valuable than it undoubtedly is at present.

Much criticism has been levelled at Interpol, particularly in recent years. This has come both from the popular press and from professional police circles but it is right to place the criticism in perspective. Interpol facilitates, co-ordinates and encourages international police co-operation among its 127 member countries as a means of combating crime. It is true that it has broadened from this basic concept in certain fields, particularly narcotics, where there is a system of liaison officers to facilitate closer international co-operation. The critics seem to blame the organisation for not living up to the fantasy image which they themselves create for it. In terms of efficiency of operation, Interpol can never be better than those law enforcement agencies which comprise it. As we have seen earlier, these agencies have problems of jurisdiction and some a parochial attitude which is regrettable but understandable.

In Europe the member states of the EEC are closely bound by economic and social legislation but other legal changes have not taken place and there is no such thing as a European Police Area. Why should this be? The answer seems to be political in that the possible loss of sovereignty in this field is unpopular. While this, the European Police Area, may be the ultimate objective, the attainment is as far distant now as it was when the Treaty of Rome was first signed.

The nearest thing we have to an international police force, or at least the principles under which one would operate, is in the United States of America. There we have State—the North American term—Forces who enforce state laws within the limits of that geographical area and a Federal or national force which is responsible for those specified as being outside the limits of state jurisdiction. The way in which this system could be applied in an international sense is somewhat clouded by the plethora of local community forces which form part of the American scene.

International Policing and the Concept of an International Maritime Bureau

Policing has always been a reactive process. The existence of a police force is evidence of that fact. Police did not exist before there were law breakers.

Once the criminal has established a new pattern of crime, police respond with a two-fold objective. The desire is both to detect the culprit and to create measures which will prevent a recurrence. These measures are aimed at straightforward crime prevention and the deterrent effect of the apprehension and punishment of the offender.

This system operates imperfectly but well enough within national boundaries where both the criminal and the law enforcement process function within one social and legal environment. When the criminal or his crime cross these national boundaries, the advantage shifts very much away from the police. Obviously, the criminal is not concerned with the variations between countries. He is acting outside the law and may be able to turn the very points of difference to the benefit of his own particular activity. The problems of the police are somewhat different. Firstly, police forces cannot have anything greater than a national jurisdiction and for all international aspects of a crime they must rely on someone else. Secondly, many countries place a different emphasis on some aspects of illegal activity. Lastly, the problem of communication is one which is still difficult to overcome.

The existence of these problems and the need to find a solution was recognised over 60 years ago when the first moves were made to set up an international police co-ordination agency, eventually to become Interpol. This organisation came into being when the prime consideration of police forces in an international context was to apprehend a fugitive offender. It is this same basic organisation which is trying to cope wih the tremendous upsurge of international criminality at the present time.

On examination, international crime in general, and maritime fraud in particular, seem to give rise to some anomalies. Recently, a senior police officer with an international awareness greater than most, said that, of over 60 suspicious sinkings reported to him, he only had jurisdiction in respect of five of them. In these circumstances there is understandable frustration on the part of commercial interests at the apparent inability or unwillingness of the police to become involved.

This same officer also referred to the lack of resources of police to undertake complicated international fraud enquiries. He referred to other demands on police time. Whether they like it or not, or whether they care to admit it or not, police are very much at the whim of public opinion which reacts more sharply against "social" crime than it does against "business" crime. Thus, if one force is faced with a serious robbery problem and a serious fraud and has to choose between the two, then it is the robbery which gets the attention because robbery is an affront to society, whereas a fraud is not. This is less than satisfactory to the victim of the fraud. What, then, are the alternatives?

If the criminal is unfettered by national boundaries in his activity, then it is only right that the investigative process should be equally free. As it will be many years, if ever, before we see an international jurisdiction, even for the major international crimes, the only possible answer to the marine fraud problem lies in a non-governmental body to get to grips with the problem. This was the idea behind the International Chamber of Commerce's International Maritime Bureau which will give the industry the opportunity to show that it can deal with its own particular problems.

International Maritime Bureau (IMB)

The objective was to provide an organisation which is flexible enough to provide a measure of response and investigative ability. It was proposed that the organisation be sufficiently close to the problem to be of commercial assistance but not too close that the business objective is the only consideration. As an overall rather than specific function, the bureau would be able to collect and collate information concerning illegal practices and trends and, thus, do two things. Firstly, it would, by dissemination of the intelligence gained, thwart future crimes and, secondly, it would formulate proposals for improved commercial practices to enable marine cargo transportation to become self-protecting.

Preliminary research has shown that, from the known instances of illegal and unethical practices, not only is it possible to provide a programme of education to prevent those in the industry from making the same mistake twice but also to identify areas for change in international commercial practice.

The IMB has now started operations in London under the direction of Mr. Eric Ellen, the co-author of this book. Its staff and consultants have been carefully selected for their wide backgrounds and range from experts on international law to ships' masters.

The prime function of the IMB is to serve as a focal point for the industry but it will also serve as a central clearing house for information. This will be made available to members in the form of various services. Once acquired, information will be collated, analysed and turned into the type of intelligence required for each service. The service available can broadly be separated into those which have a preventive function and those which have a remedial one.

Four services will be offered which have a preventive function. The first of these is an education service. Members will be able to seek advice on how to supplement their present training programmes with material on the prevention of maritime fraud. The content of such material will depend upon the requirements of each member and additional assistance will be available in its design.

The second preventive service is the provision of general information. This will be made available through the regular publication of a bulletin to allow members to keep abreast of latest developments in various parts of the world.

The third service which can be subsumed under this category will enable members to seek advice on whether potential trading partners are known to have previously been involved in fraudulent or suspect practices. Prior knowledge of this could have saved much anguish and financial hardship on numerous occasions.

The final preventive service involves authenticating trading documents for banks and others that may need such assistance.

As well as preventive services, the IMB will also offer remedial ones. The first of these is to advise and suggest avenues of procedures to those who suspect they have been defrauded.

The second remedial service is what might be termed a deviation search. A variation of cargo theft occurs when a vessel fails to arrive at its intended port of destination because the cargo has illegally been sold and off-loaded elsewhere. The name of the vessel is frequently changed at least once during this operation. The purpose of the deviation search is to locate the vessel, regardless of name change. Once located, appropriate action can be taken.

The final service which can be seen as having a remedial function are in-depth surveys into particular losses. Such surveys will enable the IMB to discover the particulars of the frauds and will also enable it to arrive at an accurate picture of the overall extent of the problem. This is something which has so far been largely guessed at. If the system currently used in international maritime trade is at fault and requires amendments, surveys of this type will provide the *International Chamber of Commerce* through the IMB with the necessary insight.

At the present time, there is no other organisation filling this need. There are a few private companies and individuals who offer a consultative or investigative service but, being commercial, they are unable to tackle the broader issues and the problems are such that collective action is called for.

There is no doubt that a problem exists. There is equally no doubt that an improvement of the situation is not only possible but essential. It is also true that the present controlling processes find it difficult to bring this about. The only possible answer is for the marine cargo industry to present a unified image and, in certain areas, to co-operate rather than compete.

It is worthy to note that, in a paper prepared for a meeting of Commonwealth Law Ministers, Barbados, April-May 1980, by Dr. Barry A.K. Rider, Fellow of Jesus College, Cambridge, President of the British Institute of Securities entitled "The Promotion and Development of International Co-operation to Combat Commercial and Economic Crime," it was proposed that a post of Commonwealth Fraud Liaison Officer be established. His tasks would include, *inter alia,* the development of criminal financial intelligence, liaison with Interpol, dissemination of information, technical assistance, co-ordination of international investigations and training.

This proposal resulted from a call from the Commonwealth Law Ministers for urgency in developing and facilitating international co-operation in regard to "white collar" crime.

It would appear that, with the commercial world working towards an International Bureau and a similar organisation for law enforcement officers of Commonwealth Countries, the problem of fraud is now receiving the attention it deserves.

An excellent example of the practical limitations placed upon the police in any form of international crime can be studied in a Hong Kong case where it was held that the disclosure of certain information between different Forces is illegal. The case came before the Hong Kong Court of Appeal, cited as *A.G. for Hong Kong* v. *Ocean Timber Transportation Ltd.* (1978) No. 86.

Very broadly, the circumstances of the matter were that the Royal Hong Kong Police were informed by the Royal Fijian Police that it was suspected that directors had conspired to defraud a Fijian company and committed theft to their detriment. A Commercial Crimes Bureau officer was granted a warrant to search the Hong Kong premises and did so, taking away a number of confidential documents which they felt would help them.

Unsurprisingly, the Fiji police officers who had supplied the initial information were anxious to be allowed to inspect copies of the seized material but were disappointed because the Hong Kong police refused, at least temporarily, to allow the documents or copies of them to leave the colony. Ocean Timber's directors applied for an order preventing the Hong Kong police from sending documents or copies to Fiji, and preventing disclosure of their contents to any person not specified in the warrant to search. The court upheld the director's application and disclosure was thereby prevented. One can see from the reported judgment that the judge had much sympathy with the police, recognising that co-operation between the forces of different territories was intended for the general public good. Against that argument, however, he felt bound to place the right of individuals to a degree of privacy about their confidential affairs, and the fact that legislation enacted in one colony could not properly take effect in another. It was never suggested that either of the two police forces were acting improperly, either in the matter under discussion, or indeed in their normal exchange of intelligence. Part of the judgment is of particular interest in this regard:

" . . . nothing I am about to say should be construed as discouraging the police from extending to their counterparts in other states, directly or through Interpol, every assistance they can, provided only that they do not put themselves outside the law of Hong Kong. As criminals seek to take more advantage of international boundaries so the need for international co-operation in fighting crime increases. Nevertheless the proviso that the police should not put themselves outside the law of Hong Kong is important . . ."

And later:

" . . . The present statutory provision allowing the issue and enforcement of search warrants is to enable the police to obtain evidence which may assist in the conviction of a person of an offence with which he is charged or reasonably suspected to be guilty. This must however be an offence triable in Hong Kong . . ."

The court went on to suggest that the time had arrived when the legislature might have to re-consider the powers open to the police in matters of this kind. Failure to recognise the dangers inherent in a situation where co-operation between police forces may be tainted with illegality can do nothing to improve channels of communication. Communication and the free exchange of information internationally, is, vital to effective effort against international criminals. The Hong Kong case is, therefore, of fundamental importance as a limiting factor in any proposed exchange of material and which its owner wishes to retain some rights of privacy and possession. Without appropriate legislation in each interested state, such problems are likely to face police forces in the future.

Intergovernmental Organisations

The United Nations

The UN came into being as a result of a series of conferences held between 1943 and 1945. A Charter of some 111 articles was drawn up at a conference held on April 25, 1945, and in October of that year instruments of notification were filed by a large number of participating members bringing the Charter into force. At its inception, six principal organs were created, namely the General Assembly, Security Council, Economics and Social Council, Trusteeship Council and the International Court of Justice. In addition to these there is the Secretariat. None of these is of particular interest within the context of this book, except in relation to the UN's role as a source of international law, and it is to commissions and intergovernmental agencies that one must look to see how and where it may have some effective influence on maritime crime.

The intergovernmental agencies—the World Health Organisation (WHO) and the International Labour Organisation (ILO) among the earliest and best known, for example—are autonomous organisations with a special relationship to the UN. They have separate budgets, executive and secretariat staff, and are not obliged to have national members in common with any other agency. The agency of special interest in the context of this book is:

The Inter-governmental Maritime Consultative Organisation (IMCO)

This agency was set up in March 1958 upon the attainment of the necessary number of States accepting the Convention agreed in 1948. The Convention required acceptance by 21 States of which at least each of seven had 1,000,000 g.r.t. registered under its national flag and with the entry of Japan that requirement was met.

IMCO's objectives are to facilitate co-operation and the exchange of technical information concerning ships and shipping practice; the encouragement of high standards of maritime safety in both operation and navigation, and the preservation of life at sea. The organisation has an Assembly as its policy making body, based in London and concerned with its budget and work programme, and a Council acting as the governing body between the biennial Assembly sessions. The third limb of IMCO is the Maritime Safety Committee whose members are elected by the Assembly for a four-year term of office.

In addition to the inter-governmental agencies, there are a number of Conferences held under the UN's auspices, two of which are of some interest. They are the United Nations Conference on Trade and Development (UNCTAD), and the United Nations Conference on International Trade Law (UNCITRAL).

UNCTAD

Of UNCTAD one need not say too much, because, quite clearly its function is primarily that of encouraging the development of trade and other matters, of which international marine carriage has a substantial part. The conference has no investigative powers other than by committee and it can do little more than examine, collate information and make agreed recommendations. The one particular matter of interest is UNCTAD's attitude to flags of convenience and in that, its efforts have been towards phasing out for political and economic reasons, rather than as a means of controlling crime. The primary proposal was that, by international agreement, open registry would be phased out by 1991 but, as so often happens in international affairs, the talks broke down, in January 1980, without a consensus. The developing nations could not agree on a common approach; Liberia, Panama and Cyprus disagreed with a Third World contention that open registry resulted in the exploitation of Third World labour, whilst some developing nations did not relish the inevitable loss of foreign currency which would result if the motion succeeded. Foreign currency sent home by nationals crewing "flag of convenience" ships is a valuable commodity to countries having exchange problems, and will not be given up lightly. UNCTAD's view when the matter first came before it was that phasing out would benefit developing countries because:

> "These countries would gain increased employment opportunities industrial diversification and the opportunity to improve their balance of payments."

One can only conclude from the final break-down of negotiations that the developing countries took a somewhat different view.

UNCITRAL

UNCITRAL would appear to be a more interesting prospect. So much maritime crime is possible because enforcement of international law is fraught with difficulty and any organisation with a responsibility for contemplating such laws is worthy of some study.

The Commission's function was first prepared in a report "The Progressive Development of The Law of International Trade," submitted to the UN General Assembly at its 21st Session in 1966. Those functions were stated to be:

> "Preparing and promoting the adoption of new international conventions, model laws and uniform laws, and the codification and wide acceptance of international trade terms, provisions, customs and practices."

Its first session was held in the spring of 1968 and Professor Schmitthoff reported that "It established, not without difficulty, the character of its work as being of a technical, non political legal nature." Here would seem to be the ideal vehicle for international efforts to reduce maritime crime through legislation, but of course one must be constantly aware of the limitations imposed upon it: those limitations common to every effort to create laws which are truly enforceable. The limitations are hinted at in the first line of its functions, "Preparing and promoting the adoption of . . . " etc., and one knows that its sharpest weapon is no more than the strong recommendation.

IMCO would seem to be the body having terms of reference sufficiently wide to play an active part in suppressing maritime crime, as well as being able to press its conclusions firmly in areas where pressure sometimes works. The most effective weapon available to IMCO is that of the Convention, which, when agreed by members, is published and offered to member states and others as a model law to be adopted in future national legislation.

An example of IMCO's activities can be seen in a Note from The Secretary-General to the Assembly, asking that its members consider a request from the Lebanese government, that "criminal barratry and the unlawful seizure of ships and their cargoes" be made subject of an item on the agenda of the eleventh session. The document discussed was as follows:

"1. *Background*

Acts of criminal barratry and unlawful seizure of ships have occurred recently as a result of the concerted action of groups of shipowners, charterers, masters, agents, merchants and so forth from various countries who agree together to divert a ship and its cargo in order to hand over the latter to persons other than the lawful consignees. Such groups use various means in furtherance of their actions including the sale of the ship, changing its name, ownership or flag, or unloading it outside authorized ports, selling the ship together with its cargo, and so forth.

Serious crimes of this kind are prejudicial to the safety of international shipping and to the legitimate interests of shippers, consignees, insurers, etc. and, furthermore, concerted action and international collaboration are necessary in order to prevent and suppress such crimes and to punish their perpetrators, a task that cannot be carried out by a single country acting on its own.

In accordance with the IMCO Convention, in particular Article 1(a), (c) and (d), Lebanon requests the Secretary-General of IMCO and the Council to examine the urgent question' of criminal barratry and the unlawful seizure of ships and their cargoes and, if possible, to include it in the agenda of the eleventh session of the Assembly, and suggests that steps be taken with a view to:

    (a) taking the requisite effective measures to prevent and suppress such actions;

    (b) referring this matter to the Legal Committee of IMCO for the preparation of an international convention for the suppression of criminal barratry and the unlawful seizure of ships and their cargoes.

Lebanon considers that such measures might be defined as set out below.

2. *Measures designed to prevent criminal barratry and unlawful seizure*

2.1. *States should be recommended:*

2.1.1. to exercise control over ships entering and leaving ports, and also to carry out a thorough scrutiny of documents relating to ships and to their cargoes and to take action against and detain any ship, Shipmaster, or other person found to be in default.

2.1.2. to exercise control over suspicious operations involving any change in the ownership, flag or name of ships, in particular when undertaken in the course of a voyage by concerns owning only one ship;

2.1.3. to recommend shipowners to take out insurance to safeguard the carriage of cargo to its destination;

2.1.4. to recommend States, in the case of decisions by the judicial authorities to distrain a cargo on behalf of a shipowner to the detriment of the charterer of the ship, that such cargo be unloaded and placed in the hands of the authorities ordering the distraint (and not in the hands of the shipowner concerned). It is also recommended that if it is decided to sell the cargo, either wholly or in part, in order to recover the freight charges, the following procedure should be adopted:

    (a) notification of the shippers of the cargo at the ports of embarkation;

    (b) notification of the consignees at the ports of destination;

2.1.5. to ensure rapid and direct communication between the maritime, customs and police authorities of the States concerned if a ship deviates from its original route, if it is in an irregular situation, if it is a fugitive or if there is any suspicious and unexplained delay in its arrival at the port of destination;

2.1.6. to advise the chambers of commerce of exporting and importing countries to exercise care in the selection of carriers;

2.1.7. to publicize the measures taken by the State concerned.

3. *Measures designed to suppress fraudulent barratry and unlawful seizure*

3.1. *At national level:*

3.1.1. the pursuit and arrest, in accordance with the terms of the applicable national and international laws, of the ship concerned in the case of fraudulent barratry, and of any person having participated in such act (shipowner, charterer, master, agent, merchant, etc.), and to impose severe penalties on them;

3.1.2. measures to restore the cargo to the rightful consignee.

3.2. *At international level* We consider that it would be useful to prepare an international convention for the suppression of criminal barratry and the unlawful seizure of ships and their cargoes along the lines of the Convention for the

Suppression of Unlawful Seizure of Aircraft concluded at the Hague in 1971. Such a convention might resolve the following problems:

3.2.1. determining the offence and also persons committing it, participating in it or acting as accomplices;

3.2.2. determining the scope of the convention and the vessels and voyages to which it applies;

3.2.3. suppressing the offence by severe penalties, treating it in the same way as piracy and authorizing the boarding of the offending ship;

3.2.4. declaring that all persons taking part in the offence are jointly and severally liable, obliging them to hand back the seized goods and to make restitution for any damage caused;

3.2.5. dealing with the question of distraint of goods as explained in paragraph 2.1.4.;

3.2.6. establishing a legal presumption of criminal barratry which admits of refutation in cases where a ship does not arrive at its destination and does not deliver its cargo and where the consignee sues in respect of non-delivery;

3.2.7. determining the law applicable to such offences, for example the law of the flag State for acts committed by the shipowner, the charterer, the master and so forth and the law of the place of unloading for acts committed by the agent, the unlawful recipient, etc.;

3.2.8. determining which States are competent to deal with the offence; such competence might be similar to that relating to the applicable law mentioned in the preceding paragraph;

3.2.9. defining the rights of the accused;

3.2.10. determining cases involving extradition;

3.2.11. affording the broadest possible reciprocal judicial assistance between contracting States in accordance with the penal procedures relating to the offence;

3.2.12. transmitting to IMCO and to Member States full information relating to the offence and ensuring the exchange of information proposed in paragraph 2.1.4.;

3.2.13. establishing procedures for arbitration and for ratifying, implementing, amending and denouncing the convention.

In conclusion, we consider that international co-operation along the lines we have explained, constitutes the best guarantee of preventing, suppressing and putting an end to these unlawful acts which jeopardize the safety of international shipping.''

The result of that document having been discussed was the passing of a resolution:

"Resolution adopted by IMCO
Assembly 15/11/1979

THE ASSEMBLY,

CONSIDERING that acts of criminal barratry and the unlawful seizure of ships and their cargoes are highly prejudicial to the legitimate interests of the owners of ships and goods, shippers, consignees, insurers and users of international maritime transport,

RECOGNIZING that an alarming increase in such fraudulent acts gravely endangers the integrity of international seaborne trade,

NOTING that urgent measures should be taken in order to attempt to prevent and suppress such acts,

RECOMMENDS that Governments, subject to applicable national and international laws, take and co-operate in appropriate legislative, administrative or other measures which could help to prevent and suppress acts involving or likely to involve barratry and the unlawful seizure of ships and their cargoes and safeguard the legitimate rights of all persons and authorities concerned,

INVITES Governments to notify the Secretary-General of measures taken by them in this respect and requests the Secretary-General to communicate such information to all Member Governments,

REQUESTS the Council to provide for a study of this matter on the basis of highest priority in order to determine the steps IMCO should take in respect of this matter and to report the results of its efforts to the twelfth regular session of the Assembly."

IMCO again discussed the problem of maritime fraud at their Council meeting held in London on June 4, 1980. It was there disclosed that replies had been received to their previous resolution for information on measures taken by members and that replies had been received from the United States, Greece and Spain. A communication had also been received from the United Nations High Commissioner for Refugees, who suggested that IMCO might also consider the effects that piracy was having on the "boat people," in South-East Asia.

The Lebanese delegation reported that it had adopted certain preventive and repressive measures and that legal action had been initiated against the author and accomplices in the criminal barratry cases which had come to light in Lebanon. In addition, draft legislation had been prepared for the suppression of criminal barratry and the unlawful seizure of ships and their cargoes. The draft text gave definitions of the crimes and the severe penalties, ranging from terms of hard labour to the death penalty in the case of shipwreck or death of individuals. The Lebanese delegation proposed to the Council that it set up a Working Party, consisting of representatives of IMCO member states and open to participation by other international bodies such as the International Chamber of Commerce, the insurers associations and others.

Mr. Rees (International Chamber of Commerce), speaking at the invitation of the Chairman, said that the ICC attached supreme importance to the question of international maritime fraud, which provided a perfect example of a field in which close international collaboration was essential if elimination of that malpractice was to be achieved. It should be noted, incidently, that as far as the ICC was concerned the term "international maritime fraud" covered a range of offences wider than the concept of acts of criminal barratry and unlawful seizure of ships and their cargoes referred to in the agenda item. In point of fact, the ICC considered that international maritime fraud had been committed whenever a party to an international maritime transaction unlawfully succeeded in extorting money or goods from one or more of the other parties. In some cases there was collusion between the parties, while in others no unlawful act was committed but one of the parties merely refrained from reporting certain information known to it. During the past three or four years, the ICC had had to take cognizance of several cases of international maritime fraud in the context of the study it had undertaken on that subject in co-operation with the national and international organisations listed in the Annex to the communication attached to document C XLIV/10/Add.1.

It emerged from the analysis of the known cases of international maritime fraud that in most incidents the ships involved had been built more than 15 years ago, carried only one type of cargo and had changed owners shortly before or shortly after the incident. Thus far, only a small number of countries had been implicated in cases of international maritime fraud, but the ICC had the impression that the number of cases was steadily increasing. Their nature, too, had somewhat changed: to begin with, they had related to the vessel itself, whereas at present it was usually a matter of falsifying documents in order to conceal the fact that no goods existed, or that they did not match up to the quality ordered by the purchaser.

The ICC took the view that at the moment the emphasis should be laid on prevention. As far as it was concerned, it would continue the activities it had already undertaken on that score, such as the organisation of meetings directed specifically towards preventing fraud and monitoring the development of the situation through the agency of its Working Party on International Maritime Fraud. It endorsed the Lebanese proposal to set up a Working Party under the auspices of the IMCO Council and was prepared to co-operate fully with IMCO in organising its meetings. The Council members were in favour of setting up a Working Party which would include all IMCO members with participation of the commercial interests and international organisations concerned.

If some positive action results form this initiative by Lebanon, a country much affected by maritime fraud, crime of all other varieties and in particular barratry, then IMCO's part in suppressing maritime crime will have been visited with a degree of success.

The International Court of Justice

The International Court of Justice sits permanently at The Hague and functions within the terms of its Statute which is an integral part of the UN Charter. Every member state within the United Nations is subject to the Statute but there is provision for non-member states to become parties to the Statute on conditions agreed by the General Assembly. There are 15 judges, all of different nationalities and each appointed following election by the General Assembly and Security Council. The method of selection for nomination is such that only candidates of proven worth in the field of national and international laws are considered, and from examination of those who have served as judges, the very best have generally been chosen.

The Court's jurisdiction may be found in Article 36 of its Statute;

1. The jurisdiction of the Court comprises all cases which the parties refer to it and all matters specially provided for in the Charter of the United Nations or in treaties and conventions in force.

2. The states parties to the present Statute may at any time declare that they recognise as compulsory *ipso facto* and without special agreement, in relation to any other state accepting the same obligation, the jurisdiction of the Court in all legal disputes concerning:

    (a) the interpretation of a treaty;

    (b) any question of international law;

    (c) the existence of any fact which, if established, would constitute a breach of an international obligation;

    (d) the nature and extent of the reparation to be made for the breach of an international obligation.

3. The declarations referred to above may be made unconditionally or on condition of reciprocity on the part of several or certain states, or for a certain time.

4. Such declarations shall be deposited with the Secretary-General of the United Nations who shall transmit copies thereof to the parties to the State and to the Registrar of the Court.

5. Declarations made under Article 36 of the Statute of the Permanent Court of International Justice and which are still in force shall be deemed, as between the parties to the present Statute, to be acceptances of the compulsory jurisdiction of the International Court of Justice for the period which they still have to run and in accordance with their terms.

6. In the event of a dispute as to whether the Court has jurisdiction, the matter shall be settled by the decision of the Court.

Article 38 defines the law to be applied by the Court:

1. The Court, whose function is to divide in accordance with international law such disputes as are submitted to it, shall apply:
>   (a) international conventions, whether general or particular, establishing rules expressly recognised by the contesting states;
>   (b) international custom, as evidence of a general practice accepted at law;
>   (c) the general principals of law recognised by civilised nations;
>   (d) subject to the provisions of Article 59, judicial decisions and the teachings of the most highly qualified publicists of the various nations, as subsidiary means for the determination of rules of law.

2. This provision shall not prejudice the power of the Court to decide a case ex aequo et bona, if the parties agree thereto.

Article 59 eloquently outlines the Court's limitations:

The decision of the Court has no binding force except between the parties and in respect of that particular case.

The Court performs a vital function in international affairs in settling disputes between states recognising its jurisdiction, but it clearly cannot act in matters where one of the parties is not subject to its jurisdiction. This latter circumstance arises in so many cases of maritime crime that the Court must almost inevitably be discounted us a useful tribunal in that field. To reinforce that view, one can make interesting comparisons between the instruments recognising the Court's jurisdiction, lodged by three quite separate and distinct nations.

"I hereby declare on behalf of the Government of Uganda that Uganda recognizes as compulsory *ipso facto* and without special agreement, in relation to any other State accepting the same obligation, and on condition of reciprocity, the jurisdiction of the

International Court of Justice in conformity with paragraph 2 of
Article 36 of the Statute of the Court.
New York, 3 October 1963.

(Signed) Apollo K. KIRONDE,
Ambassador and Permanent
Representative of Uganda to the
United Nations.

I have the honour, by direction of Her Majesty's Principal
Secretary of State for Foreign and Commonwealth Affairs, to
declare on behalf of the Government of the United Kingdom of
Great Britain and Northern Ireland that they accept as compulsory
ipso facto and without special convention, on condition of
reciprocity, the jurisdiction of the International Court of Justice, in
conformity with paragraph 2 of Article 36 of the Statute of the
Court, until such time as notice may be given to terminate the
acceptance, over all disputes arising after 24 October 1945, with
regard to situations or facts subsequent to the same date, other
than:

  (i) any dispute which the United Kingdom
       (a) has agreed with the other Party or Parties thereto to
            settle by some other method of peaceful settlement; or
       (b) has already submitted to arbitration by agreement with
            any State which had not at the time of submission
            accepted the compulsory jurisdiction of the Inter-
            national Court of Justice.
 (ii) disputes with the government of any other country which is a
       Member of the Commonwealth with regard to situations or
       facts existing before 1 January 1969;
(iii) disputes in respect of which any other Party to the dispute has
       accepted the compulsory jurisdiction of the International
       Court of Justice only in relation to or for the purpose of the
       dispute; or where the acceptance of the Court's compulsory
       jurisdiction on behalf of any other Party to the dispute was
       deposited or ratified less than twelve months prior to the
       filing of the application bringing the dispute before the Court.
The Government of the United Kingdom also reserve the
right at any time, by means of a notification addressed to the
Secretary-General of the United Nations, and with effect as from
the moment of such notification, either to add to, amend or withdraw any of the foregoing reservations, or any that may hereafter
be added.

New York, 1 January 1969.

(Signed) L.C. GLASS

I, Harry S. Truman, President of the United States of America, declare on behalf of the United States of America, under Article 36, paragraph 2, of the Statute of the International Court of Justice, and in accordance with the Resolution of 2 August 1946 of the Senate of the United States of America (two-thirds of the Senators present concurring therein), that the United States of America recognizes as compulsory *ipso facto* and without special agreement, in relation to any other State accepting the same obligation, the jurisdiction of the International Court of Justice in all legal disputes hereafter arising concerning

    (a) The interpretation of a treaty;
    (b) any question of international law;
    (c) the existence of any fact which, if established, would constitute a breach of an international obligation;
    (d) the nature or extent of the reparation to be made for the breach of an international obligation;

Provided, that this declaration shall not apply to

    (a) disputes the solution of which the parties shall entrust to other tribunals by virtue of agreements already in existence or which may be concluded in the future; or
    (b) disputes with regard to matters which are essentially within the domestic jurisdiction of the United States of America as determined by the United States of America; or
    (c) disputes arising under a multilateral treaty, unless (1) all parties to the treaty affected by the decision are also parties to the case before the Court, or (2) the United States of America specially agrees to jurisdiction; and

Provided further, that this declaration shall remain in force for a period of five years and thereafter until the expiration of six months after notice may be given to terminate this declaration.

Done at Washington this fourteenth day of August 1946.

(Signed) Harry S. TRUMAN.''

8 The Commercial Organisations

The Baltic Exchange

The Baltic Mercantile & Shipping Exchange, began in London's coffee houses, as did so many city institutions. The Baltic's principle function was to marry ships with cargoes and in the seventeenth century, coffee-house keepers provided accommodation, refreshments and information for ship owners, captains and merchants. In time, this casual arrangement for contact between interested parties became less than adequate so that a more formal scheme had to be adopted. In 1823 a body of rules was drawn up and formalities for membership of the "Baltic Club" were agreed, including a limit upon the number of members. The principle marine trade was then in tallow, vital to the manufacture of the only effective means of artificial light—candles. Later on, transport of grain began to take on greater importance until, near the turn of the century corn was the most important commodity transported by sea between England, Europe and America.

The members of the Baltic concerned with ship chartering are divided into two basic kinds, the chartering agent and the owner's broker. The chartering agent is commissioned to find space aboard suitable ships to transport a merchant's goods, whilst the owner's broker is in business to provide a suitable ship. Some of the firms having membership consist of both chartering agents and brokers so that the functions performed by the various members may appear somewhat confusing to the outsider. Business in The Exchange is not confined to United Kingdom merchants or ships but is truly international in character with either or both parties acting for principals who are neither domiciled in England nor conduct their principle business here.

As in any commercial market, buyer and seller have degrees of expertise which make highly complicated transactions appear easy. With freight rates fluctuating constantly, ships being subject to all manner of delays and accidents and a host of other variables, the task of "fixing" a single charter is difficult. When a member is representing a number of clients all with different problems, the task appears to the uninitiated to be Herculean. Elsewhere in this book one sees that not every chartering transaction takes place as the result of a "fixing" on the Baltic Exchange and one knows from experience that most cases of maritime fraud are in connection with charters arranged elsewhere. This should not, however, be seen as guaranteeing that no such frauds are committed through the medium of charters originating in the Baltic, for there are and, no matter how vigilant its members may be, there will always be. Vigilance among members is awakening as the result efforts by the Port of London Police and others, and in time the level of such crimes may well diminish into insignificance.

It would be unjust to simply dismiss the Baltic Exchange as a place whose major interest was in fixing ship charters, because its scope has widened considerably in recent years. Air charters; purchase and sale of ships; grain and cattle feed markets and a future market in wheat, barley and oil-seeds are all part of the Baltic's daily business. Coupled also with the Baltic is the Institute of Chartered Ship-brokers, many of whom hold joint membership in the exchange. This Institute is primarily for the benefit of its own members, having the task of fixing proper fees and generally promoting the efficient exercise of their work. There is, quite naturally, some advantage to clients of the Institute members since it has a standard to maintain thus guaranteeing a measurable standard of performance by those who have, by examination, succeeded in achieving membership.

The International Chamber of Commerce

The I.C.C. is an international organisation of businessmen from more than 90 countries, who have banded together to protect the private sector's interests in world trade and investment. It is non-profit making and independent of governments, but by the very weight and influence of its membership, has a valued consultative status among the authorities in most countries where there are members. The organisation was set up in 1919 in answer to a clear need for re-construction of trade which had suffered from four years of major war, by British, American and European business leaders. Its headquarters are in Paris, the home of its secretariat, but there are National Committees in more than 50 countries, both developed and developing.

As a representative organisation, the I.C.C. has Category 1 status with the United Nations Economic and Social Council, and has special rights of access to such inter-governmental bodies as UNCTAD, the World Bank, OECD, GATT and the Common Market. One can see that the scale of influence is very wide and that the I.C.C.'s council is a body to be heeded at the deliberations of the inter-governmental organisations.

The I.C.C. affairs are administered by a Council but day-to-day matters are dealt with by an Executive Committee under the control of the Secretary General. There are some 30 commissions working within the I.C.C., each having responsibility for some specialised area of international trade and each of these is made up of businessmen who are specially qualified in their field. Each nation with a significant membership has formed, or will no doubt in due course form a National Committee, through which contributions to the main body are channelled.

There are two main functions of interest in the context of this book, the first being the organisation's influence of the documentation of international trade; the second on its future role in the control and suppression of maritime crime. The I.C.C.'s contribution to documentation can best be seen in the background notes from its publications department, under the headnote *Technical Function.*

"An important part of the ICC's work is devoted to securing the adoption of agreed practices and codes of conduct which directly contribute to the facilitation of international trading. For instance, few businessmen who have been involved in international trading will be unfamiliar with the ICC's work on Uniform Customs and Practice for Documentary Credits. The rules first laid down in 1922 and recently updated for the third time (and now supplemented by a lucid and authoritative Guide) are applied throughout the world to trade transactions covered by Letters of Credit. Almost equally widely known is 'Incoterms' which provides a set of international rules for the interpretation of the chief terms used in foreign trade contracts. First produced in 1936 and subsequently revised, it is again being reviewed to ensure it keeps pace with developments in the international movement of goods. Other indispensable tools of trade for the world's business community are provided by the ICC's publications on transport documentation, collections of overseas payments, contract guarantees etc."

But what of the I.C.C.'s future in suppressing crime?

At the present time the I.C.C. is approaching the problem by instituting an anti-fraud programme, the first tangible evidence of which is found in their publication of a Guide to Fraud Prevention. This pamphlet was prepared by the I.C.C. with the aid of internationally acknowledged experts from shipping, insurance, banking and the law. The next potential weapon in the fight against fraud, is a bureau having the skill and capacity necessary to collate and co-ordinate investigations, to which reference has already been made.

The General Council of British Shipping

The G.C.B.S. is a body which came into being as recently as 1975, with the aim of representing British owners in their dealings with governments and other industries. Whilst non-political in its constitution, the G.C.B.S. negotiates wih the government on matters affecting its members and offers its assistance and advice upon appropriate matters. It is much concerned with the training, selection and recruitment of lower grade merchant seamen and has important functions connected with their welfare.

Much of the G.C.B.S.'s work is concerned with safety, research and policy making and for that reason it is of only marginal interest within the context of this book. There is, of course, the very important corollary to its work, that of receiving and disseminating information about ships and those who man them. It is in this particular area that the Council becomes of some interest, if only to make readers aware of its functions and of the potential value in situations where fraud is suspected. With its members being well represented on those organisations whose purpose and constitution have been more fully explored, there is perhaps no need to consider further the objectives of this organisation.

Lloyd's Register of Shipping

There are two matters which should be emphasised before one begins to discuss L.R. as it is being increasingly referred to: (a) the organisation's relationship to Lloyd's of London, and (b) its function as a ship classification undertaking.

L.R. sprang from the same source as Lloyd's of London, in that they both had their beginnings in the London coffee houses where merchants met to transact their business. The underwriters found it beneficial to catalogue and classify the ships they were being asked to insure and, in due course, that information began to be written up into a register of ships. In time a dispute broke out among the merchants with the result that separate registers were published in opposition to each other. In the early nineteenth century there was a reconciliation of the opposing interests, resulting in Lloyd's Register of Shipping being formed as an entirely separate entity from the insurance market. Although independent, members of the committee of Lloyd's serve on the L.R. committee and the two organisations combine for the purpose of pooling information for their computer based information service.

L.R. is essentially a ship classification and registration service and it is possible to fall into the trap of confusing national with commercial registration when considering its function. Registration with a government is required before a ship can sail under the protection of a flag, with all the advantages and responsibilities that such registration brings upon owners, master and crew. L.R. registers ships only in the sense that their details are published in the Register of Ships as a source of reference. Yet another trap into which one might easily fall is that of regarding L.R. as only a classifying or registering society. That, so far as this particular book is concerned is its most interesting function but one has to remember that there are some 1,800 L.R. surveyors around the world whose work is concerned with design, safety and progress in the building of new ships to L.R. classification. Nor is the society's activities restricted simply to ships, for as well as all aspects of ship and ship's equipment, it is intimately concerned with offshore gas and oil, as well as many land based industries.

The Register is of considerable value to those concerned with maritime crime in any form. It lists some 70,000 merchant vessels of over 100 g.r.t. and the kind of information one can derive from it is as follows:

(1) Lloyd's Register Identity number. Radio call sign. Official number. Navigational aids fitted.

(2) Ship's name. Former name, with date of change. Owner. Managers. Port of registration. National flag.

(3) Weight under the various headings i.e. Gross, net, summer deadweight.

(4) Classification into type of ship, hull, machinery and type of equipment aboard. This heading also shows the date of special surveys and its status under different classifying societies.

(5) *Hull.* Date of building. Shipbuilders and yard. Dimensions and construction materials.

(6) *Cargo capacities.* Description of ship & passenger capacity. Number of holds, tanks and their capacity. Details of hatches, winches etc.

(7) *Machinery.* Details of motive power. Engine builders. Bunker capacity and particulars of auxiliary machinery.

The register contains much more in other sections from which an enquirer can obtain sufficient information to make an informed judgment and the whole is kept up to date by the publication of periodic supplementaries showing changes.

When one reads details of some successful maritime fraud, one looks to see whether or not there was information available to the victim from which he might have at least have been put on enquiry. In most cases there was, and in very many of them the basic information from which to start an enquiry could have been found in Lloyd's Register, or by enquiry from the organisation.

A paper on the role of the Classification Societies in the field of maritime crime was presented at a conference in Hong Kong in April 1980, by Mr. R. A. Powell. In the authors' view this paper is of considerable importance and it has therefore, with consent, been included in full at Appendix D.

The Salvage Association

The Salvage Association is an agency taking a very active interest in maritime crime in whatever form it is manifested. It is right that it should be so since the Association is managed by a committee whose members are nominated by Lloyd's of London, the Institute of London Undewriters, and Lloyds Underwriters Association together with company members. The chairman of each of the nominating associations is *ex-officio* a member of the committee. The London office is managed by a General Manager with a staff of over a hundred, but there are representatives in the major ports of North America, South Africa, the Mediterranean, the Far East, England and Europe.

Formed in 1856 to look after the interests of Lloyds Underwriters, marine insurance companies, shipowners and merchants, the Association was granted its first Royal Charter in 1867 under the unwieldy but descriptive title of the *Association for the Protection of Commercial Interests as respects Wrecked and Damaged Property*. In 1971, in view of the considerable widening of its objects and interests, a new Royal Charter was granted, together with a coat of arms. In that Charter is the following definition of its objects:

" . . . the protection of any interest however arising in respect of shipping and cargoes and all matters capable of having any bearing thereon; marine, non-marine and aviation insurance and all matters capable of being the subject thereof or having any bearing thereon."

It is with the marine aspect alone that we are here concerned and it is within the Association's own booklet that one finds an extension in lay language of the objects contained within the charter.

"The Association acts largely on the instructions of Underwriters, although those instructions are so closely associated with the interests of the Assured that the Association fulfils the duty of protecting commerce in general.

The principle function of the Association is to investigate casualties in which Underwriters have an interest. Thus, when a casualty is reported and a claim seems possible, it is common practice for Underwriters to instruct the Association to act.

The Association then initiates an examination of the circumstances of the casualty and determines the extent of damage to the property subsequently providing the owner with information and recommendations for the protection and preservation of the interests of all the parties.

In cases involving survey of damage to ships and cargoes which may be subject of a claim, the Association is concerned neither with establishing or determining liability nor with deciding what may be recoverable under the policy. Its role and that of its appointed surveyors in attendance, is to establish the nature, cause and extent of the damage and to make recommendations to the parties concerned regarding repair or other means of establishing the quantum of the loss."

Typical of the Association's work is the situation wherein a ship is reported in difficulties and needing assistance from a salvage tug. Both ship owner and salvage company will welcome the advice, and often the attendance of a well qualified salvage officer from the Association's nearest office. Acting in the interests of the insurers, the Salvage Office not only tries to minimise loss, but also keeps a log of the event in order to assist in the eventual claim settlement. Another function, very relevant to these cases where fraud is a possibility, is that of inspecting hulls in a pre-insurance survey. The survey takes in all accessible areas of the ship and its machinery, with a note of relevant damage, defects or matters likely to result in trouble at some future time. The object of these surveys is to provide underwriters with an independent assessment of the risk they are being asked to cover. One can see that a potential "rust bucket" insurance fraud might be difficult to carry out where such a pre-insurance survey had been held.

Perhaps the most significant function from the point of view of those concerned with maritime crime, is the collection of information about marine casualties, for here is a potentially powerful weapon for use in prevention and detection of crime. The Association's information collation and retrieval system is a growing and highly important feature with details of several thousands of casualties being processed each year. Access to such information is vital to those whose interest is marine crime because without it, the possibilities of identifying patterns of dishonesty are few. It is only when presented with a digest of information which shows a significant pattern that interested parties can realise the full implications. The FERIT report demonstrates this very clearly and one has the impression that as soon as its compilers were able to view suspicious casualties in the Far East as a whole, any doubts they may have had about the scope of fraud were quickly dispelled. For many years policemen have recognised the individual "trade marks" of a great many habitual criminals and by recording those "trade marks" in a *modus operandi* index, have created a useful aid to detection. Such basic information is bound to lie, perhaps buried but nevertheless there in the indices of the Salvage Association, and it may be that with a growing awareness of maritime crime, a key may be forged in order to gain access to it.

Lloyd's of London

Almost from the very beginning of this book one sees that the most likely loser, except perhaps where there has been personal injury, in maritime crimes will be insurers and whenever one thinks of insurance the name of Lloyds springs at once to mind. Thus there is a very strong link between Lloyds and maritime crime, making it a matter of some interest to know something about the functions and organisation of the society. A brief historical review might be of some assistance before moving on to more recent times.

Lloyds seems to have begun in the seventeenth century when those who wanted to insure their ships and cargoes could find those prepared to underwrite the risks at one or other of the City of London coffee houses. Of these, only Edward Lloyd's has survived in history by lending its name to the present London insurance market. From small and informal beginnings, underwriters collected into more formal groups until, in 1871 the Corporation of Lloyds was incorporated by Act of Parliament, to provide premises, administrative staff and all the ancillary services required in the management of such a diverse and complicated business as insurance. The Corporation does not, and never has written insurance for that is the function of its members the Underwriters, more informally termed "names."

Lloyds is simply a market where those who wish to insure a risk may find those who are prepared to accept the risk, just as it has been since the days of Edward Lloyd. Such is the volume of transactions that all business is transacted through brokers of whom there are currently some 270 firms authorised to operate within the market. When a shipper, perhaps through a shipping agent or some other agent, needs to insure a cargo for shipment under a c.i.f. contract, the probability is that it will be arranged with one of the syndicates of "names" at Lloyds. In practical terms this means that the broker will go onto the market floor with a "slip" upon which is entered details of the risk to be underwritten. A typical slip will show details of ship, voyage, cargo and value sufficient to allow an underwriter to assess the risk he is undertaking on behalf of his colleagues (or principals if he is a syndicate manager). The degree of risk will dictate the premium, expressed as a percentage of the value to be insured, and this rate will be fixed between the broker and the first underwriter who makes him a satisfactory offer. The first underwriter writes a line, that is to say writes in the percentage of the risk he is prepared to accept on behalf of his syndicate. Let us say that the slip offers a risk involving the shipment of Khan's steel girders at a value of £1,200. The first underwriter suggests a premium of two-and-a-half per cent which is accepted by the broker as the best offer he is likely to get, and then writes a line showing that he is accepting 25 per cent of the risk. Writing a line simply means that he will scribble in his share of the risk on the slip and in a very large risk, say the oil aboard a supertanker, he may only write in a line for perhaps one per cent. The Smith/Khan transaction is quite small and the broker will then go to other underwriters who write further lines until the whole 100 per cent of risk has been accepted. When the whole risk has been accepted, and acceptance in the full legal sense is complete when the underwriter has initialled his line, the slip is used to prepare a policy which is then signed by Lloyds Policy Signing Office on behalf of the syndicates who have underwritten the risk.

Lloyds underwriters do not cover marine risks alone but such other business as they transact is clearly outside the scope of this particular work. Nor does Lloyds underwrite every marine risk for there are insurance companies outside the corporation who transact such business. It is of interest to note, however, that Lloyds' standing in the world is very high indeed with some £2,000 million per year as premium income. Also of interest is the fact that some nations require their nationals to insure with a state owned insurance company, but then re-insure the risks by having them underwritten at Lloyds.

Lloyds of London Press Ltd. is a company owned by the corporation and publishes a number of different forms of information. Lloyds List is a daily newspaper in which can be found news of general interest to those concerned with shipping, reports of sailing and arrivals, casualties to ships and aircraft. Lloyds Shipping Index lists 20,000 ocean going vessels in alphabetical order each day with not only the physical description of each, but also its current voyage and latest reported position. One can hardly think of a more useful document to the suspicious shipper or insurer being offered a "bargain" freight rate, or to a trader who is considering the purchase of cargo afloat somewhere on the world's oceans. Perhaps even more valuable is Lloyds Intelligence Service, a body of information which is available by phone, telex, cable and subsequent publication to many organisations throughout the world. The intelligence is gathered world-wide from Lloyds Agents, radio stations, rescue services, ships reports and international shipping and safety organisations. The publishers declare that the service receives over 10,000 reports a year and sends something in the order of 30,000 messages. Lloyds Weekly

Casualty Reports is a digest of much of the information contained in the preceding week's copies of Lloyds List. In addition to the above, Lloyds also publishes a large volume of material which, whilst of concern to those engaged in various aspects of shipping, insurance, commerce and law, is of little specific interest in the context of this work.

P & I Clubs

The newcomer to shipping practice may well ask why a club is included in a section which purports to cover those institutions which have at least some interest in maritime crime. The answer to this apparent anomaly is found in the purpose and constitution of the clubs themselves, and perhaps in their full title, Protection and Indemnity Clubs. The clubs, of which there are a number, are mutual insurance associations, whose membership is made up of ship-owners seeking to spread certain risks among themselves. It has been said that marine insurance consists of Lloyds, the marine insurance companies and the P & I Clubs, each having quite separate but complimentary parts to play.

In general, marine insurance through the profit-making institutions, is designed to cover risks involving hulls and cargo. A charterer seeking to sell goods abroad is bound under the classic c.i.f. contract to provide proper insurance for the cargo, and it would be a very unwise owner who failed to insure against the perils of the sea before sending his valuable ship on a voyage. Such insurances, however, leave the shipowner with fairly large gaps in cover, such as personal injury, certain crew liabilities, some collision liability and cover against damage to docks and harbour walls. It is to these risks that the shipowner turns his mind when considering membership of a P & I Club. Then too, there is a need to indemnify against such matters as fines, excess harbour dues and the like. Clubs are financed by their individual members on a pro-rata system and each is in the care of a professional manager assisted by a board of Directors drawn from among the members. A notable difference between an insurance company of Lloyds underwriter and a P & I Club is that club members tend to consult the club's managers very freely whenever in doubt about some particular aspect of their business. A result of this free consultation is that club managers have a considerable body of information at their finger tips. Quite apart from the desirability of having a general view of important institutions, the existence of this form of information is a matter of some importance to marine operations and those who are concerned with crime.

9 The London Insurance Market

The London insurance market appears to be facing an "identity crisis." Partly as a result of its own self-regulatory role and partly as a result of dislocative changes taking place in the political and socio-economic environment the world over.

The extrinsic pressures of recent times are evident in the form of growing sense of nationalism among nations which in the past had relied upon the London Insurance Market. The latest example is the setting up of insurance syndicates by the Arab states in August 1980. This was a direct response to London market's move to charge extra war risk premiums in the Arabian Gulf. Similarly, UNCTAD (United Nations Conference on Trade and Development) has criticised the English marine insurance practise over its unfair procedures which benefit the underwriters. Lately, UNCTAD has concentrated on producing a world-wide standard marine insurance policy.

Intrinsically, the disturbing events over the past few years include the *Savonita* affair which involved a fraudulent claim and the *Sasse* syndicate which exceeded its underwriting capacity. Similarly, there is a growing oligopolistic tendency in the brokers' portfolios. For example, in 1978, three broking groups had placed 41 per cent of the total premiums at Lloyd's and this was before the recent series of mergers.[1]

The above issues, coupled with the reaction of the press-media indicate that all is not well in the style and structure of the self-regulated insurance market.

With regard to the "identity crisis," one can identify the following three principle areas which need to be examined:

(1) Is the policy of "laissez faire" appropriate in the market place? Is the oligopoly in the broking business desirable?

(2) Is self-regulation/self-policing adequate to maintain the market discipline? How much governmental intervention, if any, can the market tolerate?

(3) What is the "social responsibility" of the insurance industry? What is the appropriate stance to be taken by the various sectors of the insurance market regarding changing expectations and demands made by the society?

The insurance industry has attempted to resolve the identity crisis by establishing in February 1979 a working party under the chair-

---

[1] Coppack, Lee, "Brokers Power Issue Firmly Dealt With," Lloyd's List, 27.6.80.

manship of Sir Henry Fisher. After 12 months of careful examination of the overall structure of Lloyd's, the Fisher working party's findings and recommendations were published in June 1980.[2] Briefly, the recommendations dealt with the power and discipline of brokers, Lloyd's Acts and rule-making power, the Council of Lloyd's, etc. Lloyd's has already accepted the underlying principles of Fisher report and a Bill has been placed before Parliament.

The publication of the Fisher report indicates that the London Insurance Market has seriously begun to question its fundamental nature and the market-place discipline. Such critical self-examination is a healthy sign indicating the industry's positive attitude to keep abreast of developments.

The objective assessment by the Fisher enquiry mainly deals with the first two issues of the identity crisis, *i.e.* the shortcomings of "laissez faire" atmosphere and the possible reform of self-regulatory role at Lloyd's. However, despite its broad terms of reference, the Fisher enquiry barely touched on the third issue of "social responsibility" of the insurance industry.

The question of "social responsibility" of business has been responsible for debates in academic literature. In the words of Eilbirt and Parket, this controversial issue is still "a dense thicket of conjecture."[3]

This discussion will concentrate on the above issue, fraudulent claims and their treatment by the underwriters/brokers.

At the outset it is important to clarify the meaning of "social responsibility" for, as Humble has stated, these two words can be "a semantic booby trap."[4] Here, they refer to the obligation of the insurance industry, beyond the requirements of the legal and professional codes, to appreciate the social consequences of its decisions whilst continuing to be a profitable industry.

For the purpose of this discussion, the *Savonita* affair is an interesting study. It has received wide press coverage and a debate in Parliament.[5] Judging by the press reports, it is reasonable to assume that the above affair was instrumental in initiating the Fisher enquiry. The facts, briefly, are as follows:

In November 1974 the *M.V. Savonita* sailed from Savona, Italy for the United States of America with a cargo of 2,697 motor cars, of which the majority were Fiat cars, for the American market. These

---

[2] *Self-Regulation at Lloyd's,* Report of the Fisher Working Party, May 1980.

[3] Eilbert, H. and Parket, I.R., "The Current Status of Corporate Social Responsibility" *Business Horizons,* August 1973, pp. 5–14.

[4] Humble J., *Social Responsibility Audit: A Management Tool for Survival* (London, Foundation for Business Responsibilities, 1973).

[5] House of Commons, Official Report Parl. Deb., Vol. 946, no. 86, col. 1755 (H.M.S.O.).

cars were insured with SIAT (Società Italiana—Assicurazioni Trans-porti), who in turn re-insured them in the London market through their brokers P.W.S. (Pearson Webb Springbett) and W.F.D. (Willis Faber Dumas).

After approximately eight hours sailing, a fire was discovered on the cargo deck. It was quickly extinguished but a number of cars had been damaged by fire, smoke and water. The vessel returned to Savona and unloaded 301 cars damaged during the fire. These cars were declared a "constructive total loss"[6] and sold to a Fiat dealer in Naples for approximately 15 per cent of their new value. The vessel sailed to its original destination with the balance of cars on board.

The claim was subsequently paid by SIAT on a salvage loss basis, *i.e.* the damaged cars were sold by Fiat on "as is where is" basis and SIAT paid the difference between declared value of the cars and the proceeds of their sale. SIAT made a claim upon the reinsurers through their brokers.

In January 1975, P.W.S. presented a claim for 711,643 U.S. dollars to the reinsuring underwriters. The survey reports of the claim were unsatisfactory. On May 7, 1975 the leading underwriter of the reinsurance slip instructed Graham Miller & Co. (Mr. Bishop) to make enquiries on the reinsurer's behalf. After the result of initial enquiries was made known to Mr. Pearson (Chairman of P.W.S.), he refrained from pressing the claim against reinsurers and kept the leading underwriter and IFI (parent company of Fiat) informed.

Bishop's enquiries suggested that the claim was grossly overstated. The majority of cars were found to be in near perfect condition and were reported to have been sold for 80 per cent of their new value. The method of sale was found to be highly unconventional, with a bulk of the payment being "cash," cheques. The reinsuring underwriters offered a commercial settlement of 10 per cent. of the claim, being the cost of estimated damage as found by Bishop.

P.W.S. continued to refrain from pressing the above claim for full settlement. In April 1976, SIAT dismissed P.W.S. as their brokers and transferred their account to W.F.D. including the *Savonita* claim.

In the meantime, Pearson sought advice from Mr. Mathew (a senior treasury counsel at the time) as to his position and further course of action. Mathew concluded that the evidence suggested a strong possibility of a fraudulent claim and advised Pearson that his action of not pressing the claim was the right course.

It is alleged that W.F.D. put undue pressure on the reinsurers to

---

[6] Constructive total loss in this case means the expenditure for repairs would have exceeded the repaired value of cars. For a fuller definition see Marine Insurance Act 1906, s. 60(1).

settle the *Savonita* claim. In February 1978, the claim was finally settled by the reinsurers for 96 per cent of the amount involved.

In March 1978, Mr. Aitken raised a debate before Parliament about the *Savonita* claim and the circumstances surrounding it.

In May 1978, Lloyd's appointed a committee under the chairmanship of Mr. Clifford Clark, M.C., to investigate various allegations involved in the *Savonita* affair. The relevant issues, as far as this discussion is concerned, were as follows:

(1) What is the broker's responsibility in collection of this claim?
(2) Was undue pressure applied by W.F.D. to settle the claim?
(3) What is the Lloyd's underwriter's responsibility in settlement of the claim?

The report of the *Savonita* Board of Inquiry weighed strongly against Pearson. The Report suggested that the whole affair was a "conflict of personalities." However, the Board accepted that there were undoubtedly unsatisfactory aspects to the claim. It also acknowledged the fact that on one occasion, the behaviour of W.F.D. personnel was robust beyond the normally acceptable standards of broking.

The majority of press media gave a hostile reception to the report of the *Savonita* Board of Inquiry, describing it as incomplete.[7]

On its face the *Savonita* claim involved a relatively insignificant amount. Undoubtedly, claims tainted with suspicion of fraud are not an uncommon phenomenon to the insurance industry. The alleged constructive total loss of the cars was only a secondary issue. However, the principle involved was of crucial importance, *i.e.* when a broker is presented with a claim which he honestly believes to be fraudulent, should he proceed with the settlement of the claim?

The learned opinions on this issue differ. The *Savonita* Board of Inquiry stated that the broker should inform both the parties (the assured and the underwriter) and then either go ahead with the claim or withdraw. On the other hand, the Fisher report states (13.33):

" . . . it will be always inconsistent with the Brokers duty to the Assured for him to disclose to underwriters without the consent of the assured, that he knows or suspects that a claim is fraudulent. If the Assured instructs the Broker to put forward a claim which the Broker knows or suspects to be fraudulent, it will be for the Broker to decide whether to comply with those instructions or to inform the Assured that he cannot do so (or cannot do so without disclosing his knowledge or suspicions to Underwriters). Where the Broker *knows* that the claim is fraudulent, his duty will be clear; but where he merely *suspects* and cannot, despite all proper investiga-

---

[7] For details: *The Daily Telegraph;* December 9, 1978; *The Financial Times,* December 12, 1978; *Post Magazine,* December 14, 1978; *The Economist,* December 16, 1978.

tions, discover for certain whether or not his suspicions are well founded, he will be in a dilemma to which we see no easy answer.

What is quite clear is that he has no duty or right to disclose his dilemma to underwriters—although they may draw certain conclusions if they hear that he has withdrawn."

The views expressed in the Mathew opinion (*ibid.*) are far more disturbing as evident in the following paragraph:

"However, from a strictly *legal* point of view, in so far as the criminal law is concerned, if Mr. Pearson refuses to have anything to do with the collection of the claim (as we suggest he must), he is under no further legal duty to do anything more. In other words, he is not compelled to report his suspicions to any authority, nor to take any action to see that others take no part."

Such a state of affairs must surely leave a broker in a very vulnerable position. Although he has no legal duty to report his suspicions, if a fraud is eventually proved, the broker may become party to the fraud and liable to criminal proceedings.

Under the law of Agency, as an agent of the assured, a broker is under a duty to present honestly and efficiently his clients claim to the underwriter. Similarly, the code of conduct drawn up by the Insurance Brokers Registration Panel says:

"Insurance brokers shall at all time conduct their business with utmost good faith and integrity."[8]

The decision reached in *Holland* v. *Russell*[9] states that if the broker wilfully misrepresents a material fact, he is guilty of fraud and, therefore, liable to insurers for the consequences. Similarly, the ruling in *Connecticut Fire Insurance Co.* v. *Kavanagh*[10] says that the agent of the assured employed to deal with the loss, must not either by fraud or by negligence, induce insurers to pay a loss for which to *his knowledge they are not liable*.

Let us now look at the obligations of underwriters in fraudulent claims. In the leading case of *Chapman* v. *Poole*[11], Cockburn L.J. said that in cases of suspicious claim, it is *the duty of the insurers to the public* and their shareholders, if they are a public company, to insist upon a full and searching investigation into the case. It is appreciated that the underwriters, during their course of business, encounter a number of dubious claims. In the words of a leading underwriter, "If the insurers were to investigate every 'fishy' claim, the costs involved would soon wipe them out of business."

[8] S.I. 1978 No. 1394. Schedule to the Insurance Brokers Registration Act 1977.
[9] *Holland* v. *Russell* (1863) 4 B. and S. 14; 2 New Rep. 188.
[10] *Connecticut Fire Insurance Co.* v. *Kavanagh* [1972] A.C. 473.
[11] *Chapman* v. *Poole* (1870) 22 L.T. 306.

Wider implications of the Savonita affair

As regards a broker's obligation to report suspicious claims, the Mathew opinion (*ibid.*) goes on to say:

> "We stress that there is no *legal* obligation, but we do feel, however, that Mr. Pearson has moral and business obligations, that he will be concerned as to his good name and reputation in the London Insurance Market, and that he will feel that he has a duty not only to protect the good name of Lloyd's and the Institute but also see that other reputable brokers are aware of the dangers to them in pursuing the claim."

The above issue of "moral obligations" takes us into the much debated areas of management style, company ethos and the social responsibility of the business mentioned earlier.

Traditionally, a firm's responsibility was to carry out its economic functions and stay within the law. This view is inadequate in today's dynamic business environment. As people become better off materially, they aspire to a better quality of life, better business ethics, etc. A typical example is of the "Thalidomide" incident in the early 1970s. In this respect the editorial in *Management Today* (December 1972) had said:

> " . . . It is true sadly, that businesses do sometimes behave in ways which in a private individual would be considered despicable, even criminal."

In some respects, the wider issues of the *Savonita* affair have a degree of similarity to the "Thalidomide" incident, *i.e.* a conflict between private gain and public duty—should a broker pursue a fraudulent claim bowing to commercial pressures or should he resist and hope that in the long run "good ethics is good business"?

With regard to the duty to disclose fraudulent claims, if not legal, then as said by Cockburn L.J. (*ibid.*) it is a public duty. In this context it is interesting to note the views of the Confederation of British Industry. In the words of C.B.I. company affairs committee:

> "The law sets minimum standards of conduct, but it does not, and can not, embody the whole duty of man; and mere compliance with the law does not necessarily make a good citizen or a good company."[12]

Despite the growing involvement of Government in business, the insurance industry has enjoyed freedom of self-regulation. Professional codes and self-regulation are appropriate if the business is

[12] Confederation of British Industry, *The Responsibility of the British Public Company*, Final Report of the Company Affairs Committee, 1973.

treated as a game, where players follow the unwritten rules. However, the indications are that, in recent times, some of the players in the insurance game have not kept to the rules. The Fisher Report stresses the fact that a club atmosphere is inappropriate in present times and the implied rules, *per se,* are not sufficient for maintaining trust for the market.

If the insurance industry is not to lose its freedom to legislation, then it should be capable of self-reform. As mentioned earlier, the Fisher report has set the wheels in motion. However, the key issue, in the context of fraudulent claims, remains unresolved, *i.e.* the disclosure of suspicious claims to law enforcement authorities. One effective weapon to contain frauds is to publicise the co-operation between the insurers and the authorities which would act as a deterrent to offenders. A classic example is the FERIT investigation[13] which resulted in a reduction of frauds in that region.

Maritime fraud is probably the latest addition to non-tariff distortions towards international trade. Recently the Saudi Arabian ban on vessels passing through Lebanese ports bears out the above contention. With the growing concept of free trade and an increase in the exchange of secondary and tertiary products, the number and complexities in frauds are likely to grow unless checked. If the frauds continue the ultimate result will be higher premiums on hull and cargo and the imposition of a hidden tax on the consumer—the end user of shipping services. The key, in the form of co-operation with the authorities, lies in the hands of the insurance industry and all the other innocent parties caught up in frauds.

The discussion began with the identity crisis in the London Insurance Market. Only the issue relating to fraudulent claims has been considered.

The *Savonita* affair is an interesting study. The burnt-up cars and the claim were minor issues. The case is important since it brought out the wider issues of public duty and a possible reform in professional codes.

---

[13] Far East Regional Investigation Team (FERIT) was set up under the auspices of the Salvage Association to investigate a rising toll of vessels foundering in the South China Sea. The co-operation with the police, particularly in Hong Kong and Singapore, was commendable. During its four month undercover inquiry in 1979, FERIT produced detailed documentary evidence on the extent of frauds in the area.

10 Prevention of Maritime Fraud

Crime has long been with us and cargo has always had a special attraction to the criminal. This is particularly true of those who can use the system without being directly involved themselves.

Marine cargo handling is an evolving process and in present day international maritime trade, the unscrupulous appears to be able to practise his art with little danger of discovery or retribution. At least this was true until until quite recently when both governments and industry itself began to sit up, take notice and encourage positive action.

The opportunities given to the fraudster and the controlling process have made the problem enormous in both size and effect. But it is compounded by the fact that the ordinary citizen does not see its consequences as affecting him directly, with the result that he does not use his public voice to demand the measures that would give him protection.

It will be shown that maritime fraud does work to the detriment to the man in the street, and why he, with his better-informed brothers and sisters in shipping, should use all possible endeavours to have it brought to an end.

In Chapter 4 the various types of fraud were placed into categories and an explanation of each was given within a legal context. Here, the same frauds will be discussed, but in a wider social, economic and commercial connection.

Documentary Fraud

Documentary fraud is both complex and simple. The commercial details of international trade documentation make the fraud and associated forgery a complex proceeding, but generally there are only two main parties involved, the buyer and the seller, so that simplicity lies in the absence of the multiplicity of characters which typify a charter-party fraud.

At a seminar on the Prevention of Shipping Fraud held in New York in June 1980, Judge Charles S. Haight of the United States District Court, Southern District, New York, said of Documentary Fraud:

"The shipping industry is particularly vulnerable to documentary fraud because a single transaction can involve actors in several different countries. Where geographical distance is great, and personal participation minimal, reliance upon documents is commercially essential, but the system is obviously vulnerable to fraudulent manipulation.''

Trade and trust used to be almost synonymous terms, but it seems that the increase of the former has resulted in a decrease of the latter. Perhaps this is because in earlier years trade was hard won and easily lost, whereas in more recent times there has been a dramatic extension of trading possibilities into areas in which a corresponding growth of trading morality has not been a natural process.

The time and distance involved in marine cargo transportation make a system of payment before delivery essential. One of the two parties, either the supplier or the receiver, must for a time, have neither money nor goods, and a system has evolved in which it is the receiver who finds himself in this state. This convention has given rise to the letter-of-credit system. Operated between men of honour this system has stood the test of time, and still operates fairly in the vast majority of cases. However, the unscrupulous have found that they can turn the system to their own advantage.

The distance separating the parties means that an intermediary must be involved and this is normally a bank. The buyer who, after all, is placing his money at risk, nominates a bank to pay the money to the supplier once certain preconditions have been satisfied. These revolve around the transference of documents, because documents can be transmitted faster than the goods to which they refer. It is because documents are the linch pin of the operation that forgery has become a factor in this type of crime. Since time immemorial anything that has value has attracted the forger's art, and a bill of lading can be a lot easier to forge than the Mona Lisa but just as lucrative.

The paying bank has to be satisfied that the consignor who is seeking payment has satisfied the conditions set up by the consignee. There are two areas of difficulty, however, one avoidable, the other, unfortunately, not.

In the first area buyers are often very naive about the conditions they set (in one case the buyer authorised the bank to pay on the production of ten different documents. This would seem prudent—but closer examination showed that every one of the 10 documents originated from the seller or the seller's agents, so that not one was of independent origin). It is difficult to ascertain why this is so. It could be that the buyer is pleased to get goods in a sellers' market and fears that if he made problems over payment he might lose the opportunity to buy.

The second area, in which it is difficult to make improvement, is with the banks. Codes of practice will be referred to later, but some banks are a little less than willing to accept instructions with a letter of credit that would require them to make any enquiries out of the ordinary. This attitude is understandable, to a degree. Banks deal with letters of credit by the thousand, and to vary conditions for a few would make the whole system most unwieldy.

There are many instances on record where the most elementary precautions could have prevented the loss of a great deal of money. There have been cases where cargo has been offered on the commodity markets as being on board and at sea though a check of the vessel's name against the port of loading would have shown that the vessel had been thousands of miles away from that port on the date in question. It is astonishing that neither the forger nor the victim checks these facts. With this lack of attention to detail there is no wonder that sometimes a forged bill offers a quantity of cargo which exceeds the displacement tonnage of the vessel supposedly carrying it.

If it is possible to check the authenticity of documents, on whom should the responsibility fall? One could be excused for thinking that as the bank is the point of exchange then it is there that the problem should rest. Unfortunately, this is not so. Banks abide by the "Uniform Customs and Practice for Documentary Credits" issued by the International Chamber of Commerce. Articles 8 and 9 state:

(8) In documentary credit operations, all parties concerned deal in documents and not in goods.

(9) Banks assume no liability or responsibility for the form, sufficiency, accuracy, genuineness, falsification or legal effect of any documents.

So banks have little if any responsibility for their actions or the consequences of any shortcomings in what they do. Why should this be? Banks will argue that they deal with many thousands of letters of credit each year and that the percentage of fraud is very low indeed. With this there can be no argument; but it is cold comfort to a victim who has lost many thousands of pounds to know that he is only a small percentage.

There seems to be scope for a two-level operation on the part of the banks. For the routine operation trading along a well trodden path there should be a low-security operation with a correspondingly low charge, while for those who need it there should be an operation with a much higher security-consciousness, for which an appropriately high charge would have to be paid. It is not true, however, that banks are never victims of maritime fraud.

In a recent federal case in New York, a bank was the victim of fraudulent shipping documents. Judge Meskill said in the Court of Appeals:

"This case grows out of a massive fraud perpetrated upon the National Bank of North America by Tidal Marine. The scheme was simplicity itself. Tidal was in the business of owning ships, a business universally carried on with borrowed money. The principal security for these borrowings is a mortgage on the ship itself and an assignment of the charters entered into between the shipowner and the shippers who actually operate the boats. By forging the purchase documents and charters for much of its fleet, and through the bribery of lending officers at N.B.N.A., Tidal was able to borrow vast sums of money, approximately thirty million dollars, on the strength of wholly inadequate security. When the scheme finally was revealed, it resulted in bankruptcy of Tidal, several civil actions for fraud and this prosecution."

Although basically a letter-of-credit system operates between buyer and seller there are many agents involved, and so the transactions can be not only international but multinational, with all the inherent investigative and jurisdictional problems this can bring.

As regards insurance, in some cases the cargo underwriter will take the view that under the policy the goods were never at risk. This is obviously the case in documentary frauds where the bills of lading, invoices, certificates of origin, etc., are forged. If the goods did not exist there is nothing to which the insurance cover can be attached and the Underwriters will decline liability under the policy.

From a preventive point of view there are no problems which are insurmountable. It only remains for commercial practices to update themselves, to realise that the trusting world of a few years ago no longer exists, and protect themselves accordingly.

Charter-Party Fraud

Charter-party fraud is fraud by the charterer against the shipowner, the shipper, or both. Changes in shipping patterns of recent years, and the ageing and obsolescence of some vessels, have provided a fertile base for this type of crime. Many such vessels are in the hands of small owners ready for voyage charter. They are ideal and economic for short-haul international runs, particularly in areas where physical development is outstripping the development of normal commercial practice. The unethical or fraudulent operator will charter such a vessel, paying the minimum charge necessary, sell the cargo space, collect freight charges, and see that the vessel is loaded and on its way to its destination. When the second or subsequent hire charge becomes due to the shipowner it is found that the charterer has disappeared into the air from which he came, and there are no funds.

The issue is now so complex and the motivations of the various parties other than the charterer are all so equally understandable that the problem becomes difficult. The shippers who are the wholly innocent parties in the transaction, except for their imprudence in accepting cut-price freight or other "advantage," want their goods to reach their destination. The importer, having paid for the goods, wants to see them, and the owner, sometimes the master of his own vessel, finds that he has insufficient funds to complete the voyage and pay his way with wages, bunkering, port dues and the rest.

These problems have been resolved in various ways. Sometimes the shippers will agree to pay a freight surcharge in order to get their goods to destination, and put the whole thing down to experience. Sometimes they will agree to a diversion and a sale of the goods to cover costs, and then start the export process all over again. Sometimes, however, no such compromise can be reached or even be attempted, and the master/owner will divert his ship and sell the cargo wherever he can, and thus become as much a criminal as the charterers who precipitated the whole state of affairs. The legal proceedings can then become endless wrangles, with the liability for loss usually shared by the separate parties.

As with documentary fraud, these situations can be avoided by exerting more commercial prudence than is now usual. The attitude that "my word is my bond" which used to be the bedrock of much commercial practice unfortunately is no longer common enough to be relied upon for general practice.

The 'Rust-Bucket' or Scuttling Fraud

This always involves "barratry." The word, which has long been resting in lawyer's archives, has been brought to light of day by practices which are becoming almost commonplace.

Again the breeding-ground has been the surfeit of older, out-of-date ships flooding the market. These fall into the hands of small owners or "singletons" to whom the prospect of a greater income from insurance than from lawful trade is compellingly attractive. These ships will often load freight which is of more value than the vessel itself and set sail. Some time later the crew, having had miraculous escapes, will all be rescued and tell tales of tremendous storms and mysterious explosions which caused their vessel to be a total loss. All too often enquiries show that the vessel called into an unscheduled port, discharged, and sold her cargo on the quay before slipping her moorings and putting to sea for her appointment with the storm or explosion.

The ease with which this crime can be committed comes about more by accident than design. Some ports have a history of congestion, with vessels lying outside waiting for a berth for six months or more. What starts as cargo theft from boredom becomes cargo theft to pay expenses. It is but a short step then to realisation of the potential of the "total loss."

Current developments are showing that this crime is no longer restricted to the older, smaller ship. Nor need the shipowners or charterers be totally innocent, which seems to remove some cases from the definition of barratry. Nothing prevents the practice from being extended to a bigger vessel where it is necessary to remove evidence of some other malpractice. This type of activity has become so common as to cause action by the Inter-Governmental Maritime Consultative Organisation (IMCO), which in November 1979 (see Chapter 7) adopted an emergency resolution urging action at government level to regularise national and international law to help combat the menace.

Areas of political instability offer themselves to those who engage in this form of crime. Not only does the instability make for economic pressures and demand for goods at short notice, but it also makes any form of law enforcement or control less effective. Just such a situation led an exporter from a Mediterranean country into an experience which, quite apart from the financial loss involved, could surely count as the most frustrating experience of all time. He chartered a small vessel to take a cargo of cigarettes for the one-day voyage across the Mediterranean. When the ship did not arrive on time the exporter chartered an aircraft and searched the area. He found the ship hove to on the high seas surrounded by dhows from the Red Sea, and could see his cigarettes being lowered over the side. Then the dhows put into another Mediterranean country in the grip of internal strife almost amounting to civil war, and the chartered vessel disappeared. To add final insult to injury, the exporter had the doubtful pleasure of being able to buy a pack of his own cigarettes from a street trader and not being able to do a thing about it.

Piracy

Another result of political instability is a resurgence of piracy. The cutlass and cannon may well have been exchanged for the radar and turbine but the result is the same: high-seas robbery. There is no reason to suppose, however, that this type of maritime crime will become a great problem.

Who Pays

Whether it be in the field of large-scale maritime fraud or the more parochial one of inflated damage claims, the breakdown in trading standards can be analysed as having two roots. Firstly, the overall volume of world trade, not necessarily all marine, is increasing at a great rate, and what was once particular is now run-of-the-mill, and familiarity breeds contempt. Secondly, there are very many trading areas which have gained operational autonomy before they have learned the basic principles of international trade.

It would be fair to ask who loses as a consequence of all this crime and malpractice. At first sight it seems not to be individuals, because the crimes cause only passing interest, if they achieve any publicity at all, and the losers are identified by the man in the street as "big business," who can afford it anyway. It is true that the immediate losers are usually the insurers, the shipping companies, the individual importer/exporters, the shipowners, or even the state. But such is the nature of trade that the loss does not stop there. Today's loss becomes tomorrow's surcharge, and in the final analysis, it is the consumer who pays, because he is the last in the chain of those to whom the burden of the increase can be passed. This is the ultimate in domino effects.

The Future

It has been shown that the small seedlings of criminal propensity have matured rapidly in the ideal conditions provided by international trade today. The unknown of 20 years ago became the unusual within a decade but has grown to be commonplace now. It will remain so and even increase further unless something is done. Little enough can be done to influence the trading climate. A period of recession seems almost inevitable, as does world inflation, and both these factors undermine any attempt to establish stability.

Moreover, what now exists in the marine field will certainly come to exist, if it does not already, in aviation transport. Experts have declared documentary fraud to be impossible with air freight because the airway bill is not negotiable in the same way as a marine bill of lading. This is only partly true, and, in any event, it only waits for the introduction of a system by which these documents can be transmitted more quickly than the goods to which they refer for the first aviation fraud to become an accomplished fact.

Given that we can do nothing to affect a world climate in which fraud can exist, what are the options? We can suffer in silence, or we can make a conscious effort if not to rectify the situation then at least to keep it in manageable bounds.

The conscious effort towards control can only come from two sources. Those who have the foresight to realise that they are potential victims must exercise far more care than they have done up to now. This implies no criticism of them, because it is human nature to assume that disasters will always happen to someone else, but the experience of so many must prompt others to beware. Sometimes awareness itself will not be enough, because there are so many who appreciate that something has to be done but lack the experience that would show them what their own course of action should be. The intervention of a specialist organisation is becoming essential.

For a problem so complex there can be no simple panacea, and it must be tackled at all levels. This need raises the task above the capability of a commercial organisation and places it at the level of an organisation which, while having a practical commercial approach to the various questions, is nevertheless of sufficient influence to present corrective measures to government.

Fraud Prevention

All parties should protect themselves by being extremely careful when dealing for the first time with unknown persons and by making enquiries as to the standard and integrity of the persons before entering into a binding agreement.

In particular, a cargo-owner should deal only with reputable shipowners and charterers. If a charterer is not known to him he should check with Lloyd's Register as to whether a vessel "is in class," has capacity and then with Lloyd's Shipping Index as to her position. On many occasions the vessel quoted has not been in a position to fulfil the obligation. The cargo-owner should be wary if the freight rate is too attractive. This can be explained away, but even more caution should be shown if the vessel is owned by a single shipowning company, is more than 15 years old and has passed through various owners. If a cargo-owner is uncertain he really must go elsewhere or suffer the consequences.

The following check-list probably represents an idealism that cannot be achieved in a real world but nevertheless the reader is pointed in the right direction and he will be able to modify his requirements according to his own assessment of the risks involved in the transaction.

Precautionary measures

Embassy commercial sections and Chambers of Commerce make traders aware of the risks in trade and shipping transactions. They make a minimum series of checks before advancing the names of potential suppliers, buyers or transport companies.

CIF buyers (a) Insurance should be effected through a reputable organisation under a known and accepted policy.

(b) method of payment should be against letter of credit and all the documents that must be presented for payment to be made should be indicated with adequate but not extraneous detail.

(c) shipment of the goods should be encouraged by conference lines or national lines vessels with a maximum age of 15 years; if no such vessel is available then at least seven days notice should be given to the letter of credit opener and paying bank nominating the carrying vessel.

(d) Conference or national lines bills of lading should be used and marked "Freight Prepaid" with the amount of the freight clearly stated on the bill of lading.

(e) an agent of the forwarding agent at the loading or discharge ports who is a member of a national association should be appointed to protect the buyer or letter of credit opener's interest.

(f) a survey or pre-inspection of the goods should be carried out by independent inspectors, who are not connected in any way with the buyer or seller.

(g) buyers should attempt to identify whether the carrying vessel is on charter and who the charterers and owners are; sellers should take similar precautions.

(h) when chartered tonnage is used, traders should insist on chartering only via agents of reputable institutions and allow these agents to appoint agents at the loading and discharging ports.

Agents (a) should advise shippers and receivers of any time-bar in relation to cargo claims.

(b) should aid the trader in making any checks on the particulars, charterers and owners of the carrying vessel.

Banks (a) should be encouraged to make use of Lloyd's Register and Lloyd's Shipping Index and made their documentary credit departments aware of these publications. The important points to check with regard to the carrying vessel are ownership, size and position of the vessel at the time the bill of lading was dated.

(b) if such checks are considered difficult for a bank because of the volume of work perhaps a "super-service" at an added cost should be considered with the actual checks being carried out by brokers or agents retained at an annual fee.

(c) should examine ways of improving documentary credit operations by the application of computerised and modern business methods.

Shipping companies (a) should tighten up their bill of lading departments and consider the use of an embossed coded number on each bill of lading at least for high-valued or large parcels of cargo.

Vessel owners and charterers (a) charterers should know the disponent owners or be able to check on their record.

(b) the owner should specify in the charter-party that bills of lading can only be signed by the master.

(c) in the charter-party the vessel's call-sign should be stipulated as well as the voyage plan, including bunker calls.

(d) the master should be instructed to radio his position through certain periods of the voyage and possibly, for valuable cargoes, be bound to report to the Lloyd's Agent at each port of call giving his E.T.A. at the next port.

(e) port agents should be put in funds prior to the vessel's arrival.

(f) charterers, even if using a reputable broker, should insist during negotiations that the broker/agent receives written authority to sign the contract on behalf of the owner principal.

(g) whenever possible, owners should insist that two to three months charter-hire be paid in escrow or alternatively that a Bank guarantee be delivered to them on signing the charter-party covering estimated hire.

Maritime and port authorities should prevent voyage termination unless the owner deposits with reputable agents money for onward carriage together with all other handling and insurance expenses.

All trading countries (a) should consider the tightening-up of
  (i)   transfer of ownership
  (ii) transfer of flag
  (iii) ship registration
  (iv) court proceedings which allow only one party to dispose of cargo should be prevented, *i.e.* no *"ex ante"* Court hearings should be allowed.

(b) should consider the effect of voyage deviation when carried out for reasons that are not immediately clear and proper.

Deviation plays an important part in the commission of so many maritime crimes that it warrants consideration quite separately from those crimes which have been classified under four main headings. An aircraft setting out on a flight must follow a pre-arranged flight plan notified to the air traffic control authorities through whose areas it intends to pass. The reasons why are obvious, for to set out across busy commercial or military air lanes, in and out of traffic control zones, would be to invite disaster. It may be said that there is good argument for the deposit of sailing plans by those using congested sea lanes such as the Dover Straits, but there is no such requirement. Attempts to regulate sailings on a voluntary basis have been strongly resisted, even where the arguments put forward concerned the ship's own safety. One ought here to draw a distinction between liner and tramp operations, however, because the liner does sail to a pre-determined time and pre-arranged route. This planning is not as a result of an over-riding authority having ordered it to be so, but because liner operations are required to conform for wholly commercial reasons. Properly regulated liner services sail at the advertised times whether fully loaded or not and, subject to unavoidable delays, will arrive at the advertised port. Long deviations without pressing reasons would disrupt all-important schedules and where the line has a mail contract bringing with it a measure of prestige, disruption and delay could be commercially unfortunate. In general, a liner will only make a diversion for reasons of saving life.

Tramp ship operation is in a quite different category because, whilst a tramp might make many voyages over a route with almost liner-like regularity, it might just as possibly make unscheduled diversions during the course of every journey. Deviation is an integral part of tramp ship operation, dictated by its owner or manager for proper commercial reasons. Take for example a tanker loaded in the Gulf with crude oil purchased by a charterer and being transported, notionally, to Europe. The charterer, taking advantage of the market, sells the oil whilst still afloat, to a West African buyer, to whom the oil is then diverted. The ship's Master may well have expected to sail to a European port in the same way that he had done on earlier occasions, but will hardly be surprised to find himself instructed to sail south instead of north when clear of the Mediterranean. Such a deviation will be catered for in the charter party either:

(a) being there specifically set out, or
(b) being in the course of a generally accepted trade practice, and
(c) only then by the shortest practicable route.

The sanction against unwarranted diversion under a charter-party is that the charterer may repudiate the contract contained within it. Thus a ship-owner or manager who allows his ship to be diverted to a charterer's detriment without a warranted reason, risks having the contract repudiated, with such financial penalties that result falling upon him. Warranted and justifiable deviations are well illustrated in part of the judgement in *Scaramanga* v. *Stamp* (1880) 4.C.P.D.316:

"Deviation for the purpose of saving life is protected, and involves neither forfeiture of insurance nor liability to the goods owner in respect of loss which would otherwise be within the exceptions of 'perils of the seas.' And as a necessary consequence of the foregoing, deviation for the purpose of communicating with a ship in distress is allowable, inasmuch as the state of the vessel in distress may involve danger to life. On the other hand, deviation for the sole purpose of saving property is not thus privileged, but entails all the usual consequences of deviation. If, therefore, the lives of the persons on board a disabled ship can be saved without saving the ship, as by taking them off, deviation for the purpose of saving the ship will carry with it all the consequences of an unauthorised deviation. But where the preservation of life can only be effected through the concurrent saving of property, and the bona fide purpose of saving life forms part of the motive which leads to the deviation, the privilege will not be lost by reason of the purpose of saving property having formed a second motive for deviating."

In this case, the steamship *Olympias* carrying a cargo of grain, went to the aid of another steamer which had broken down through engine failure in calm weather. There would have been no difficulty in removing the crew, but the master of the *Olympias* agreed to tow the other ship into the Texel for a fee of £1,000. Nearing port, the *Olympias* was stranded on a sand-bank and both ship and cargo were lost.

Deviation for criminal purposes is an unjustified deviation in similar form to that resulting in the case of *Scaramanga* v. *Stamp* having, at least in theory, the same potential consequences. It is of little value to the victim of fraud, however, to discover that he has a remedy in law of the same effectiveness as that available in a non-criminal dispute. Ideally, any deviation carried out for criminal purposes ought to have attached to it some kind of effective sanction but, and here one is immediately confronted with the old problem of international law: there is none that can be applied at the present time. An excellent suggestion was mooted at the Shipbroker seminar in 1979, when Mr. D. E. D. Prentice said:

> "All maritime authorities and port authorities should prevent voyage termination unless the ship-owner deposits with reputable agents money for onward carriage together with handling expenses and insurance for cargo in transit. It would be better between maritime countries to prevent voyage termination and allow the same only in connection with *force majeure*."

Perhaps this is a first step towards control of wrongful deviation, because the object of taking a ship from its planned route will usually be to terminate the voyage where the goods are to be stolen or otherwise criminally used. If effective agreement against such voyage terminations were universally applied, it follows that deviation would be difficult and indeed pointless to ports whose authorities subscribed to the suggestion put forward.

Unless and until some such agreed policy is brought into being, there is something that can be done. Perhaps the most effective action currently possible is the education of those concerned towards reporting any suspicious deviations to one of the agencies concerned with collating marine intelligence. It may be that at least some losses might then be prevented and some thieves brought to justice. With wakening interest in maritime crime it may be possible, in time, to persuade the maritime nations of the advantages which may be gained from legislation aimed at criminal deviation.

The Way Ahead—the Role of Governments—Future Patterns of Maritime Fraud

The role of governments

Before governments can be expected to initiate any special measures against maritime fraud, they must come to recognise the particularly serious nature of the problem. Governments have a specific obligation to attempt to eradicate all criminal activities within their territorial jurisdiction and it is in their own interests to do so as rapidly as possible in the case of maritime fraud.

The potential costs to government cannot be exaggerated and one has ony to recall the Costa Rican Coffee Fraud in 1959, which shook the foundation of the nation's economy and the political embarrassment of South Africa in the "Salem" case of 1980, to appreciate the economic and political influence of the larger maritime frauds.

In almost all cases of fraud government loses some revenue. It is the victim of the fraud who suffers the trading loss but as this usually means a drop in trading profits, there is a consequent reduction in its liability for corporate tax.

In the case of illegally off-loaded cargoes, government is deprived of the customs duties which should have been paid. In Lebanon, for example, this loss is estimated at £500,000 annually because of ships off-loading at Jounieh and other similar unofficial ports. Moreover, such illegally off-loaded goods inevitably find their way on to the black markets. Governments are then deprived of revenue from sales taxes. More significantly, the establishment or expansion of a country's black market seriously erodes the authority of government. Once a black market is consensually legitimised by the populace, less reliance is placed on government to provide for every-day needs and more on obliging illegal traders.

The American attempt in 1980, following the persistent detention of their diplomatic staff in Iran,to bring about an international trade boycott of Iran has brought about a new and flourishing trade in that country of consumer and luxury goods banned by the Iranian Government. The Government has reacted by ordering all imports to be dealt with through a new governmental agency and has prohibited trading by the private importer.

One shipowner in the Far East believes that there will be a marked decrease in scuttlings and other maritime frauds in 1980 and beyond. "Freight rates are too good," he says, "and smuggling is more profitable anyway."

It is often the smuggling that provides the climate in which fraudsters revel. Far from enjoying a reduction in fraud, it is more likely that there will be an increase in fraudulent transactions and variations of the basic types of deception as the perpetrators become more and more sophisticated.

First and foremost, therefore, is the need for governments to be made aware of the seriousness of the problem.

Closely allied to this is the need to make governments realise that their adoption of some simple practical measures against maritime fraud can have a disproportionately positive impact. There will, of course, be financial costs involved but these are minute compared to potential losses. Moreover, most of these costs will be underwritten by the industry in the form of higher corporate taxes from the increased trading profits which are bound to result.

The question of what governments can do in response to maritime fraud is perhaps not very appropriate. Government can, technically, legislate into existence anything it desires. What is more appropriate is to ask what practical measures governments are likely to adopt. Regardless of the severity of the problem, no government is likely to adopt or even consider any measure without taking into account the prevailing political mood in the country at the time. Neither is government likely to adopt any measure which, if it failed in its desired effect, might cause them embarrassment. Similarly, any measure under consideration by governments must be consistent with the social norms and values of the country. They must be formulated in accordance with several basic rules or principles if public trust and confidence in government is to be retained.

One such principle is a firmness and determination to uphold constitutional authority and the rule of law. Any decision on which measures to adopt and how they are to be implemented must remain the sole purview of those democratically elected to fulfil this function. Vigilante action by the industry must not be allowed and must firmly be resisted. Neither should measures be decided upon by special governmental departments invested with unlimited powers and no public accountability. Moreover, any measure decided upon must be within the law and the due process of law must be maintained. Government must also be seen to be doing all in its power to protect and safeguard the public's interests and property. Yet, despite all this, measures must be adopted which are effective.

The measures which are finally adopted will have evolved from a number of factors, such as the Government's previous experience and current abilities; its desire to be seen as supporting some specific regional or international norm or value, such as taking a resolute stand against crime or supporting the lawful possession of things; the necessity of satisfying long-term economic and political goals with the exigencies of the moment; the perceptions and personalities of key governmental decision-makers and their concomitant desire to increase personal status and self-esteem; an appreciation of the public's and the industry's demands for action and an estimation of what measures they will accept and tolerate; as well as a basic recognition of the general principles outlined above.

Nonetheless, it is possible to suggest some simple practical measures which governments might be willing to adopt. This list is not intended to be exhaustive but rather illustrative. Above all, governments must have the political will to act, must also be willing to improvise their response within the framework of the restrictions outlined above.

(1) *Creation of national task forces to combat maritime fraud.*

At present, there is little co-operation and virtually no co-ordination between the various governmental departmets which have a role to play in combating maritime fraud. Information or expertise available within one department or agency is rarely available or even offered to others. Similarly, the various parties involved in international maritime trade (*i.e.* buyers, sellers, shipowners, charterers, masters, insurers, bankers and brokers) possess intimate knowledge of their part of the trading system wherein a fraud may occur. Yet they too are rarely approached for their specialised expertise. Moreover, the various components of the system are frequently in direct opposition to governments, especially when it concerns governmental intervention or regulation of trading practices. The industry may refuse or even be unable to co-operate with governments for fear of establishing a precedent which may later be used by government to further regulate or attempt to regulate maritime trade.

A task force established at the national level with representatives of both government and industry would help to overcome these problems. It would be able to draw upon all available sources of information and expertise for the common good. Greater utilisation would thereby be made of existing resources. This would represent an immediate saving in economic cost as well as a saving in the time it would take for the task force to come on stream with an equally proficient staff.

The task force should not function as a mere clearing house for information on maritime fraud but should rather serve as a co-ordinating centre. It should be empowered to co-opt members of industry whose special expertise may be required for a specific case. Personnel and reports from various government departments or agencies which may have a bearing on maritime fraud should also be placed at its disposal. For example, commercial attachés in British Embassies overseas are well placed to report on local trading conditions and practices. They can also readily authenticate any trading document which concerns their area. Similarly Lloyd's Agents are present in every port and file regular reports of shipping movements, which can be collated and compared with similar reports provided by the Ministry of Defence and more especially by Naval Intelligence.

Special attention should be paid by the task force to any patterns or characteristics which appear to be emerging from incidents of maritime fraud. Once a profile is established, this should be disseminated to the industry at large to enable it to take suitable precautions. Such a profile will also aid the task force in its prime function; the prevention and detection of maritime fraud. Finally, once a maritime fraud is detected, the task force should have the trained personnel available to conduct the necessary investigations and be empowered to make the arrests.

(2) Creation of a central clearing house for the authentication of documentation

Documentary frauds can frequently be detected by a few simple telephone calls. In other cases, more detailed checking may be required. However, no such facility currently exists which would be able to authenticate various trading documents. Chambers of commerce may be responsible for authenticating certificates of origin but usually do not have the expertise to detect forgeries. Neither do they have the facilities nor contacts to enable them to be kept abreast of the latest techniques being used to forge documents. No central clearing house could be expected to check on the genuineness or otherwise of the millions of shipping documents in circulation daily and any attempt to do so would result in additional unacceptable costs and unreasonable delays.

In certain circumstances, however, documents could be passed through an organisation such as the International Maritime Bureau with a condition to this effect being inserted in the letter of credit.

An illustration of how prior thought and infinite care can enable a purchaser to protect himself is the case of the Asian exporter, living and working in the Far East, who purchased 10,000 tons of Thai rice which he intended to export to Nigeria. He went to his bank to open a letter of credit and there met friends who warned him that ships were disappearing in the region and particularly so off West Africa. Heeding the warnings, he related his fears to his bank manager and told him that he wanted to protect himself by entering a number of conditions in the letter of credit. He was strongly advised by the manager not to open a complicated letter of credit because of the practical difficulties the bank would experience in checking the compliance of the conditions and it was then decided that a simple letter of credit be opened. However, among the conditions of the letter of credit was a requirement that the beneficiary produce a certificate from the Asian exporter to the effect that all the terms and conditions of the contract had been fulfilled.

It was in the certificate that the Asian exporter set out in detail the conditions to be fulfilled by the seller and the beneficiary of the letter of credit. They were:

(1) satisfactory evidence of permission having been arranged for the ship to be chartered to enter Nigerian territorial waters and for such ship to be allowed berthing facilities within 5 days of the arrival of the ship in Nigerian territorial waters. (This was to ensure that the goods were discharged within reasonable time after the ship left Bangkok.)

(2) To ensure that the ship to be chartered was seaworthy, that the owners of the ship were reliable and financially sound and also to ensure that the ship did not abscond with the cargo and to ensure that insurance risks involved in the chartering a ship could be covered within a reasonable rate, it would be required within a reasonable time, allowing at least 15 days to cover such risks, the following information and documents:

    (a) the full name and address of the owners of the ship and also their bankers from whom a status report could be obtained.

    (b) name of the ship and all the normal description and specification of the ship, including name of the master of the ship.

    (c) an authenticated copy of the charter party agreement entered between the Asian exporter and the owners of the ship to be chartered. Copy of the agreement need not disclose rate of such charter. Such charter agreement would, however, have to contain satisfactory evidence on the following matters:

        (i) the route the chartered ship will take after leaving Bangkok.

        (ii) the duration of the voyage to Lagos/Apapa.

(iii) the ports of call on its route. The number of days required by the ship to reach the destination.

(iv) prohibition for the chartered ship to call at any other port either to take the cargo or discharge the cargo.

(v) a valid and binding arrangement whereby the ship would continue to supply information every third day as to their position at sea.

(vi) telex information of their position every day when the ship is three days away from the port of Lagos.

(vii) name and address of agents in Lagos.

(3) In the event of the ship not getting berth within a reasonable time of its arrival in Nigerian territorial waters satisfactory evidence would have to be produced to show there had been adequate financial provision for the ship to continue to wait for the discharge of the cargo as long as it were necessary. In other words, that adequate financial provision had been made so that the ship did not leave without discharging the cargo in the event of some dispute arising between the charterer and the ship owners.

(4) The charter party agreement should also clarify that all charges to be borne by the ship owners or charter for dues under this contract were adequately provided for.

(5) To enable a Lloyd's surveyor for inspection of the cargo to be appointed, notice should be received of at least 15 days before the ship was due to take the cargo for loading to enable provision or arrangement for inspection of the cargo by Lloyd's surveyor to be made.

The seller, perhaps not surprisingly, backed away from the deal and it was only later that the Asian exporter discovered that the rice did not exist and the whole transaction was fraudulent. By taking special precautions he had saved himself a fortune.

(3) *Publicity and education*

A third measure governments can readily adopt concerns publicity and education. Conferences and seminars should regularly be held to ensure that industry is fully aware of the problems involved in maritime fraud. It must be shown how, by taking a number of simple precautionary measures, it can generally escape being defrauded. The industry should also be kept up to date on any new developments in maritime fraud, such as changes in the profile mentioned above, as well as up to date on any new techniques of forging documents.

All investigations into cases of maritime fraud should also be publicised for two prime reasons. First, public trust and confidence in Government will be retained as the public will be able to see that government is doing all in its power to protect and safeguard their interests and property. Secondly and perhaps most importantly, publicity has an undeniable deterrent value. The severe penalties involved shoud be stressed, as should the notion that government is able to detect attempts at maritime fraud and always arrests those responsible.

Nonetheless, maritime fraud is a crime of international dimensions. No one Government will ever be able unilaterally to act against it with any lasting effect. Greater regional and international inter-governmental co-operation is needed for this to be accomplished. Here again, however, it is possible to suggest numerous practical measures which governments might be likely to adopt at both regional and international levels. For example:

(4) *Creation of national task forces by all 21 Member States of the Council of Europe*

National task forces along the lines suggested above should be created by each of the 21 Member States of the Council of Europe. These should function as the sole governmental department to be responsible for combating maritime fraud within their respective countries.

All 21 task forces should closely co-operate with each other. Information of both a substantive and technical nature should be exchanged as and when it becomes available only. Personnel should also be exchanged to allow each task force to appreciate the special difficulties or problems likely to be encountered by other task forces. One of the benefits to be gained from this is the establishment of personal contact between the various task forces. This will be of help in ensuring that co-operation will be forthcoming whenever the need arises.

(5) *Establishment of "hot-lines"*

The establishment of hot-lines between the H.Q.s of the various national task forces or between the police departments responsible for investigating maritime fraud may be of use once a specific problem is encountered and information or co-operation is urgently needed.

(6) *Establishment of a computer conferencing network*

Benefit may also be found in establishing a network between computer storage facilities of the various task forces or police agencies. Information on file with one agency in, for example, Cyprus would thereby be available to police in, for instance, the Netherlands. The computer network now in use by the various branches and levels of the West German police might serve as a useful model.

(7) *Adoption of plans for standardisation of documents*

West European governments should agree to a plan for the standardisation of documents used for maritime trade. Closely allied to this is the need to safeguard the storage of these documents from theft. Moreover, special attention should be paid to ensure that documents are only issued to the rightful person or company and that they are not readily amenable to fraudulent use. This may necessitate a re-designing of some of the documents.

(8) *Adopt an unequivocal stand against maritime fraud*

The 21 Member States of the Council of Europe could adopt an unequivocal stand against maritime fraud. They could also adopt a common plan for combating fraud and agree to co-operate more closely towards that end. Moreover, other States could be invited to adopt a unified position against maritime fraud.

(9) *Bring pressure to bear on states which are less vigilant*

Economic and political pressure could be brought to bear on states which are less vigilant in combating the problem. There are various ways this could be achieved but the most effective would be the use or the threat to use sanctions against defaulting states. Negative sanctions involve the withdrawal or denial of access to a specific product or service. If a defaulting state does not take immediate, effective action against maritime fraud, then negative sanctions could be brought against them. The most common form of negative sanctions are trading restrictions or even boycotts of specific states. Another form of negative sanction is the refusal to grant economic assistance or aid. However, negative sanctions are rarely successful, as recent experience in Rhodesia and South Africa illustrates. The boycotted state can usually find another source of goods. However some companies frequently continue to trade illegally but under a changed corporate name. A trade boycott also affects the economy of the state imposing the boycott, particularly where they are dependent upon foreign exports. If foreign orders cannot be found or are cancelled by Government, trading profits may decline. A refusal to grant economic aid may also be counter-productive. It may alienate the boycotted state and make the re-establishment of normal relations following the withdrawal of the boycott more difficult.

A greater measure of success is likely to be achieved by the use of positive sanctions. If a defaulting state agrees to adopt measures against maritime fraud, then it should be rewarded by increased trade or aid. This will have a positive affect upon the home economy. For example, Somalia had previously been used by the Palestinians as a base from which they launched the Entebbe hijacking. However, during the *Mogadishu* hijacking, the West German Government was able to prevail upon Somalia to change its attitude towards the use of terrorism by offering increased economic aid. Somalia, in turn, granted permission for the West German GSG-9 unit to mount a rescue mission.

However, international relations are geared towards the threat system and negative sanctions rather than the reward system and positive sanctions. It will, therefore, take greater political will and determination to adopt such a measure but the evidence so far is that it is likely to be of more success.

(10) *Enact new international legislation*

States could also study the possibility of proposing and enacting new international legislation against maritime fraud. However, any international legislation takes time to become effective and indeed only becomes international law through the passage of time and continued evidence of its use. International conventions, on average, enter into force roughly 10 years after they were first proposed. Such a time-scale is inapplicable here. Resolutions, on the other hand, are much more immediate. They represent a declaration of intent and are binding upon states which voted in favour.

As an initial step, therefore, a resolution needs to be proposed to the Consultative Assembly of the Council of Europe which would embody the basis of Western Europe's response. It should "call upon" Member States to do everything possible to combat the crime within their jurisdictions. It should "recommend" the Member States adopt a common plan of action, perhaps including some of the measures suggested above. It should also "recommend" the Com-

mittee of Ministers of the Council of Europe to establish a committee
of experts to study the ways and means of combating maritime fraud.

Finally, such a resolution should "urge" Member States to apply
economic and political pressure to states which are less vigilant in
combating maritime fraud. This type of resolution can also be submitted as a proposal to IMCO and the UN General Assembly for
their consideration and eventual adoption.

Although this is only a first step, it would be an important one and
would have to be followed up by other, similar resolutions as need
demanded. Moreover, once the committee of experts was established
by the Committee of Ministers and met to carry out its mandate, new
recommendations would be put forward. These, in turn, should be
included in its final report and in future resolutions.

(11) *Ratify existing international legislation*

Finally, governments of Western Europe could urge states which have
not yet done so to ratify the High Seas Convention of 1958 and other
existing international conventions which relate to maritime fraud. It
is not generally recognised that the International Convention on
Civil and Political Rights and the Council of Europe Convention for
the Protection of Human Rights and Fundamental Freedoms are
applicable to some aspects of maritime fraud. For example, when a
ship is intentionally scuttled for the insurance money, the crew's lives
may be at risk; their inherent right to life and security of person is
therefore jeopardised. This is in contravention of Articles 9(1) and
5(1) of the Conventions above, respectively. States should ratify existing international legislative instruments such as these and, more
important, amend national legislation accordingly.

There are, as can be seen from the above, numerous practical
measures which governments might be likely to adopt against
maritime fraud. The specific measure which is finally adopted, however, is less important than a government's determination to tackle
the problem. Once governments are aware of the extent and potential consequences of continuing acts of maritime fraud, Governments
will also come to recognise it is in their interests to take immediate,
action against it. Indeed, once identified, a problem is half-way to
being solved.

The future pattern of maritime fraud is very difficult to forecast
with any degree of confidence, bound as it is to be influenced by the
future of international trade. Extensive and deep recession has
resulted largely from increases in oil prices, whilst the shattering
effect of these increases upon national economies has surprised most
economists. A fall in exports from many trading nations coupled

with the lack of demand in those nations for imported goods has had its effect on shipping. Available tonnage greatly exceeds the goods for shipment in most classes of shipping with the result that many vessels are being laid up as an alternative to operating at or near to financial loss. Containerisation, nearing its peak of development, has had a profound effect upon shipping practices. In one sense it has reduced crime simply because pilferage has been substantially reduced. In another sense it has helped criminals who have been able to acquire their ill gotten gains neatly packaged and in substantial quantity.

Yet another factor must be the rise of some nations and the decline of others. Who can forecast with confidence what position Nigeria, for example, will have as an economic power by the year 2000? Who could give a reliable estimate of the United Kingdom's power to influence world events and hence world trade by then?

Of one thing we can be assured: the people who have hitherto organised maritime frauds will continue to do so, changing and adapting their methods to take advantage of circumstances as they arise. It hardly needs saying that those who have an interest in preventing loss by crime, or who are charged with the task of prosecuting the fraudsmen will have to change and adapt with the same facility.

Appendix A: The Hague Rules

The Hague Rules have the force of law by virtue of the Carriage of Goods by Sea Act 1971, in respect of goods shipped from a United Kingdom port. "The Rules" means the International Convention for the unification of certain rules of law relating to bills of lading signed at Brussels on August 25, 1924 as amended by the Protocol signed at Brussels on February 23, 1968. The following is a précis of those rules.

Article I

   (a) "Carrier" includes an owner or charterer who enters into a contract of carriage with a shipper.

   (b) "Contract of carriage" applies only to contracts covered by a bill of lading or similar document of title, so far as it relates to carriage of goods by sea. It also includes a bill of lading or similar issued under a charter party.

   (c) "Goods" includes all merchandise, etc., except live animals and goods stated on the bill of lading to be deck cargo, if so carried.

   (d) "Carriage" includes time when loaded until time discharged.

Article II

The custody and care of goods shall be subject to the responsibilities and liabilities, rights and immunities within the remaining articles.

Article III

The carrier shall before and at the beginning of the journey exercise due diligence to:

1.   (a) Make the ship seaworthy.
       (b) Properly man, equip and supply the ship.
       (c) Make the holds, etc. fit and safe for the goods to be carried.

2. Properly load, discharge and care for the goods.

3. Issue the shipper a bill of lading showing:
   (a) The leading marks necessary for identification of goods.
   (b) Quantity of the goods by weight, number of packages, etc.
   (c) The apparent order and condition of the goods.

4. Such a bill is prima facie evidence of receipt by the carrier of the goods described therein.

5. The shippers shall be deemed to guarantee to the carrier the quantity, weight, number of the goods shipped.

Article III continues with a number of rules concerning other indemnities and associated matters which are of only passing interest to the main work.

Article IV

1. Neither carrier nor ship shall be liable for loss or damage arising from unseaworthiness unless due to lack of diligence on the part of the carrier to make it seaworthy and to properly man and equip it.

2. Neither ship nor carrier shall be responsible for loss or damage arising or resulting from:
   (a) Act, neglect or fault of master, mariner, pilot or servants in the navigation or management of the ship.
   (b) Fire, unless caused by actual faulty or privity of the carrier.
   (c) Perils, dangers, accidents of the sea or other navigable waters.
   (d) Act of God.
   (e) Act of war.
   (f) Act of public enemies.
   (g) Arrest or restraint of princes, rulers or people, or seizure under legal process.
   (h) Quarantine restrictions.
   (i) Strikes or lockouts.
   (j) Act or omission of the shipper or owner of the goods.
   (k) Riots and civil commotions.
   (l) Saving or attempting to save life at sea.
   (m) Wastage in bulk or weight, or any other loss or damage arising from inherent defect of the goods.
   (n) Insufficiency of packing.
   (o) Insufficiency of marks.
   (p) Latest defects not discoverable with due diligence.
   (q) Any other fault arising without actual fault of the carrier, etc.

3. The shipper shall not be responsible for loss or damage sustained by the carrier or the ship arising or resulting from any cause without the act, fault or neglect of the shipper, his agents or his servants.

4. Any deviation in saving or attempting to save life or property at sea or any reasonable deviation shall not be deemed to be an infringement or breach of these Rules or of the contract of carriage, and the carrier shall not be liable for any loss or damage resulting therefrom.

Appendix B

LINER BILL OF LADING Page 1

(Liner terms approved by The Baltic and International Maritime Conference)
Code Name: "CONLINEBILL"

Amended January 1st, 1950, August 1st, 1952, January 1st, 1973, July 1st, 1974, August 1st, 1976, January 1st, 1978

1. Definition.
Wherever the term "Merchant" is used in this Bill of Lading, it shall be deemed to include the Shipper, the Receiver, the Consignee, the Holder of the Bill of Lading and the Owner of the cargo.

2. General Paramount Clause.
The Hague Rules contained in the International Convention for the Unification of certain rules relating to Bills of Lading, dated Brussels the 25th August 1924 as enacted in the country of shipment shall apply to this contract. When no such enactment is in force in the country of shipment, the corresponding legislation of the country of destination shall apply, but in respect of shipments to which no such enactments are compulsorily applicable, the terms of the said Convention shall apply.
Trades where Hague-Visby Rules apply.
In trades where the International Brussels Convention 1924 as amended by the Protocol signed at Brussels on February 23rd 1968 - The Hague-Visby Rules - apply compulsorily, the provisions of the respective legislation shall be considered incorporated in this Bill of Lading. The Carrier takes all reservations possible under such applicable legislation, relating to the period before loading and after discharging and while the goods are in the charge of another Carrier, and to deck cargo and live animals.

3. Jurisdiction.
Any dispute arising under this Bill of Lading shall be decided in the country where the carrier has his principal place of business, and the law of such country shall apply except as provided elsewhere herein.

4. Period of Responsibility.
The Carrier or his Agent shall not be liable for loss of or damage to the goods during the period before loading and after discharge from the vessel, howsoever such loss or damage arises.

5. The Scope of Voyage.
As the vessel is engaged in liner service the intended voyage shall not be limited to the direct route but shall be deemed to include any proceeding or returning to or stopping or slowing down at or off any ports or places for any reasonable purpose connected with the service including maintenance of vessel and crew.

6. Substitution of Vessel, Transhipment and Forwarding.
Whether expressly arranged beforehand or otherwise, the Carrier shall be at liberty to carry the goods to their port of destination by the said or other vessel or vessels either belonging to the Carrier or others, or by other means of transport, proceeding either directly or indirectly to such port and to carry the goods or part of them beyond their port of destination, and to tranship, land and store the goods either on shore or afloat and reship and forward the same at Carrier's expense but at Merchant's risk. When the ultimate destination at which the Carrier may have engaged to deliver the goods is other than the vessel's port of discharge, the Carrier acts as Forwarding Agent only.
The responsibility of the Carrier shall be limited to the part of the transport performed by him on vessels under his management and no claim will be acknowledged by the Carrier for damage or loss arising during any other part of the transport even though the freight for the whole transport has been collected by him.

7. Lighterage.
Any lightering in or off ports of loading or ports of discharge to be for the account of the Merchant.

8. Loading, Discharging and Delivery
of the cargo shall be arranged by the Carrier's Agent unless otherwise agreed.
Landing, storing and delivery shall be for the Merchant's account.
Loading and discharging may commence without previous notice.
The Merchant or his Assign shall tender the goods when the vessel is ready to load and as fast as the vessel can receive and - but only if required by the Carrier - also outside ordinary working hours notwithstanding any custom of the port. Otherwise the Carrier shall be relieved of any obligation to load such cargo and the vessel may leave the port without further notice and deadfreight is to be paid.
The Merchant or his Assign shall take delivery of the goods and continue to receive the goods as fast as the vessel can deliver and - but only if required by the Carrier - also outside ordinary working hours notwithstanding any custom of the port. Otherwise the Carrier shall be at liberty to discharge the goods and any discharge to be deemed a true fulfilment of the contract, or alternatively to act under Clause 16.
The Merchant shall bear all overtime charges in connection with tendering and taking delivery of the goods as above.
If the goods are not applied for within a reasonable time, the Carrier may sell the same privately or by auction.
The Merchant shall accept his reasonable proportion of unidentified loose cargo.

9. Live Animals and Deck Cargo
shall be carried subject to the Hague Rules as referred to in Clause 2 hereof with the exception that notwithstanding anything contained in Clause 19 the Carrier shall not be liable for any loss or damage resulting from any act, neglect or default of his servants in the management of such animals and deck cargo.

10. Options.
The port of discharge for optional cargo must be declared to the vessel's Agents at the first of the optional ports not later than 48 hours before the vessel's arrival there. In the absence of such declaration the Carrier may elect to discharge at the first or any other optional port and the contract of carriage shall then be considered as having been fulfilled. Any option can be exercised for the total quantity under this Bill of Lading only.

11. Freight and Charges.
(a) Prepayable freight, whether actually paid or not, shall be considered as fully earned upon loading and non-returnable in any event. The Carrier's claim for any charges under this contract shall be considered definitely payable in like manner as soon as the charges have been incurred.
Interest at 5 per cent., shall run from the date when freight and charges are due.
(b) The Merchant shall be liable for expenses of fumigation and of gathering and sorting loose cargo and of weighing onboard and expenses incurred in repairing damage to and replacing of packing due to excepted causes and for all expenses caused by extra handling of the cargo for any of the aforementioned reasons.
(c) Any dues, duties, taxes and charges which under any denomination may be levied on any basis such as amount of freight, weight of cargo or tonnage of the vessel shall be paid by the Merchant.
(d) The Merchant shall be liable for all fines and/or losses which the Carrier, vessel or cargo may incur through non-observance of Custom House and/or import or export regulations.
(e) The Carrier is entitled in case of incorrect declaration of contents, weights, measurements or value of the goods to claim double the amount of freight which would have been due if such declaration had been correctly given. For the purpose of ascertaining the actual facts, the Carrier reserves the right to obtain from the Merchant the original invoice and to have the contents inspected and the weight, measurement or value verified.

12. Lien.
The Carrier shall have a lien for any amount due under this contract and costs of recovering same and shall be entitled to sell the goods privately or by auction to cover any claims.

13. Delay.
The Carrier shall not be responsible for any loss sustained by the Merchant through delay of the goods unless caused by the Carrier's personal gross negligence.

14. General Average and Salvage.
General Average to be adjusted at any port or place at Carrier's option and to be settled according to the York-Antwerp Rules 1974. In the event of accident, danger, damage or disaster before or after commencement of the voyage resulting from any cause whatsoever, whether due to negligence or not, for which or for the consequence of which the Carrier is not responsible by statute, contract or otherwise, the Merchant shall contribute with the Carrier in General Average to the payment of any sacrifice, losses or expenses of a General Average nature that may be made or incurred, and shall pay salvage and special charges incurred in respect of the goods. If a salving vessel is owned or operated by the Carrier, salvage shall be paid for as fully as if the salving vessel or vessels belonged to strangers.

15. Both-to-Blame Collision Clause. (This clause to remain in effect even if unenforcible in the Courts of the United States of America).
If the vessel comes into collision with another vessel as a result of the negligence of the other vessel and any act, negligence or default of the Master, Mariner, Pilot or the servants of the Carrier in the navigation or in the management of the vessel, the Merchant will indemnify the Carrier against all loss or liability to the other or non-carrying vessel or her Owner in so far as such loss or liability represents loss of or damage to or any claim whatsoever of the owner of the said goods paid or payable by the other or non-carrying vessel or her Owner to the owner of said cargo and set-off, or recouped or recovered by the other or non-carrying vessel or her Owner as part of his claim against the carrying vessel or Carrier. The foregoing provisions shall also apply where the Owner, operator or those in charge of any vessel or vessels or objects other than, or in addition to, the colliding vessels or objects are at fault in respect of a collision or contact.

16. Government directions, War, Epidemics, Ice, Strikes, etc.
(a) The Master and the Carrier shall have liberty to comply with any order or directions or recommendations in connection with the transport under this contract given by any Government or Authority, or anybody acting or purporting to act on behalf of such Government or Authority, or having under the terms of the insurance on the vessel the right to give such orders or directions or recommendations.
(b) Should it appear that the performance of the transport would expose the vessel or any goods onboard to risk of seizure or damage or delay, resulting from war, warlike operations, blockade, riots, civil commotions or piracy, or any person onboard to the risk of loss of life or freedom, or that any such risk has increased, the Master may discharge the cargo at port of loading or any other safe and convenient port.
(c) Should it appear that epidemics, quarantine, ice - labour troubles, labour obstructions, strikes, lockouts, any of which onboard or on shore - difficulties in loading or discharging would prevent the vessel from leaving the port of loading or reaching or entering the port of discharge or there discharging in the usual manner and leaving again, all of which safely and without delay, the Master may discharge the cargo at port of loading or any other safe and convenient port.
(d) The discharge under the provisions of this clause of any cargo for which a Bill of Lading has been issued shall be deemed due fulfilment of the contract. If in connection with the exercise of any liberty under this clause any extra expenses are incurred, they shall be paid by the Merchant in addition to the freight, together with return freight if any and a reasonable compensation for any extra services rendered to the goods.
(e) If any situation referred to in this clause may be anticipated, or if for any such reason the vessel cannot safely and without delay reach or enter the loading port or must undergo repairs, the Carrier may cancel the contract before the Bill of Lading is issued.
(f) The Merchant shall be informed if possible.

17. Identity of Carrier.
The Contract evidenced by this Bill of Lading is between the Merchant and the Owner of the vessel named herein (or substitute) and it is therefore agreed that said Shipowner only shall be liable for any damage or loss due to any breach or non-performance of any obligation arising out of the contract of carriage, whether or not relating to the vessel's seaworthiness. If, despite the foregoing, it is adjudged that any other is the Carrier and/or bailee of the goods shipped hereunder, all limitations of, and exonerations from, liability provided for by law or by this Bill of Lading shall be available to such other.
It is further understood and agreed that as the Line Company or Agents who has executed this Bill of Lading for and on behalf of the Master is not a principal in the transaction, said Line, Company or Agents shall not be under any liability arising out of the contract of carriage, nor as Carrier nor bailee of the goods.

18. Exemptions and Immunities of all servants and agents of the Carrier.
It is hereby expressly agreed that no servant or agent of the Carrier (including every independent contractor from time to time employed by the Carrier) shall in any circumstances whatsoever be under any liability whatsoever to the Merchant for any loss, damage or delay arising or resulting directly or indirectly from any act, neglect or default on his part while acting in the course of or in connection with his employment and, but without prejudice to the generality of the foregoing provisions in this clause, every exemption, limitation, condition and liberty herein contained and every right, exemption from liability, defence and immunity of whatsoever nature applicable to the Carrier or to which the Carrier is entitled hereunder shall also be available and shall extend to protect every such servant or agent of the Carrier acting as aforesaid and for the purpose of all the foregoing provisions of this clause the Carrier is or shall be deemed to be acting as agent or trustee on behalf of and for the benefit of all persons who are or might be his servants or agents from time to time (including independent contractors as aforesaid) and all such persons shall to this extent be or be deemed to be parties to the contract evidenced by this Bill of Lading.
The Carrier shall be entitled to be paid by the Merchant on demand any sum recovered or recoverable by the Merchant or any other from such servant or agent of the Carrier for any such loss, damage or delay or otherwise.

19. Optional Stowage. Unitization.
(a) Goods may be stowed by the Carrier as received, or, at Carrier's option, by means of containers, or similar articles of transport used to consolidate goods.
(b) Containers, trailers and transportable tanks, whether stowed by the Carrier or received by him in a stowed condition from the Merchant, may be carried on or under deck without notice to the Merchant.
(c) The Carrier's liability for cargo stowed as aforesaid shall be governed by the Hague Rules as defined above notwithstanding the fact that the goods are being carried on deck and the goods shall contribute to general average and shall receive compensation in general average.

ADDITIONAL CLAUSES
(To be added if required in the contemplated trade).
A. Demurrage.
The Carrier shall be paid demurrage at the daily rate per ton of the vessel's gross register tonnage as indicated on Page 2 if the vessel is not loaded or discharged with the dispatch set out in Clause 8, any delay in waiting for berth at or off port to count. Provided that if the delay is due to causes beyond the control of the Merchant, 24 hours shall be deducted from the time on demurrage.
Each Merchant shall be liable towards the Carrier for a proportionate part of the total demurrage due, based upon the total freight on the goods to be loaded or discharged at the port in question.
No Merchant shall be liable in demurrage for any delay arisen only in connection with goods belonging to other Merchants.
The demurrage in respect of each parcel shall not exceed its freight.
(This Clause shall only apply if the Demurrage Box on Page 2 is filled in).
B. U.S. Trade. Period of Responsibility.
In case the Contract evidenced by this Bill of Lading is subject to the U.S. Carriage of Goods by Sea Act, then the provisions stated in said Act shall govern before loading and after discharge and throughout the entire time the goods are in the Carrier's custody.

Page 2

LINER BILL OF LADING   B.L No.

Shipper

ONE,TWO SHIPPING CO LTD
7 Eleftherias Street
ANTWERPEN
Netherlands

Reference No.

101/AP

Consignee

THREE,FOUR Confectionary Ltd
8 Sklavias Road
LAGOS
Nigeria

Notify address

FIVE,SIX Confectionary Ltd
123 Sweet tooth Industrial Estate
LAGOS
Nigeria

Pre-carriage by*	Place of receipt by pre-carrier*
Vessel m.v. "ANAX"	Port of loading Antwerp
Port of discharge	Place of delivery by on-carrier*

Marks and Nos.	Number and kind of packages; description of goods	Gross weight	Measurement
1000 Bags ABC 3333 LAGOS	"French white crystal" sugar packed in polythene bags of 25 Kgs. nett each. Nett: 25,000 Kgs.	25,008 Kgs.	

Particulars furnished by the Merchant

Freight details, charges etc.

SHIPPED on board in apparent good order and condition, weight, measure, marks, numbers, quality, contents and value unknown, for carriage to the Port of Discharge or so near thereunto as the Vessel may safely get and lie always afloat, to be delivered in the like good order and condition at the aforesaid Port unto Consignees or their Assigns, they paying freight as indicated to the left plus other charges incurred in accordance with the provisions contained in this Bill of Lading. In accepting this Bill of Lading the Merchant expressly accepts and agrees to all its stipulations on both pages, whether written, printed, stamped or otherwise incorporated, as fully as if they were all signed by the Merchant.
One original Bill of Lading must be surrendered duly endorsed in exchange for the goods or delivery order.
IN WITNESS whereof the Master of the said Vessel has signed the number of original Bills of Lading stated below, all of this tenor and date, one of which being accomplished, the others to stand void.

Daily demurrage rate (additional Clause A)

* Applicable only when document used as a Through Bill of Lading

Freight payable at	Place and date of issue
Destination	Antwerp 10/10/80
Number of original Bs'L	Signature

<table>
<tr><td colspan="2">

1. Shipbroker

Messrs. ANGELS Ltd
37 Hippo Rd.

</td><td colspan="2">

RECOMMENDED
**THE BALTIC AND INTERNATIONAL MARITIME CONFERENCE
UNIFORM GENERAL CHARTER (AS REVISED 1922 and 1976)
INCLUDING "F.I.O." ALTERNATIVE, ETC.**
(To be used for trades for which no approved form is in force)
CODE NAME: "GENCON"   Part I

</td></tr>
<tr><td colspan="2"></td><td colspan="2">

2. Place and date

GENOA 8/2/52

</td></tr>
<tr><td colspan="2">

3. Owners/Place of business (Cl. 1)

Messrs. Aquarius Ltd, New York USA

</td><td colspan="2">

4. Charterers/Place of business (Cl. 1)

Messrs. Anonymous Ltd., Russis

</td></tr>
<tr><td colspan="2">

5. Vessel's name (Cl. 1)

"ANAX" - Italian Flag
Built 1970   Class ABC

</td><td colspan="2">

6. GRT/NRT (Cl. 1)

1D 801/NRT 7 630 BREADTH 74'

</td></tr>
<tr><td colspan="2">

7. Deadweight cargo carrying capacity in tons (abt.) (Cl. 1)

20,000 LT DW Summer on 31' 3.1/4"
5 Holds/5 Hatches - Grain Cubic Capacity
in holds:855 876 cft 10 Gears of 10 T. Speed
about 14 knots on about 28T

</td><td colspan="2">

8. Present position (Cl. 1)

Now Trading

</td></tr>
<tr><td colspan="2">

9. Expected ready to load (abt.) (Cl. 1)

15 Feb 1952

</td><td colspan="2"></td></tr>
<tr><td colspan="2">

10. Loading port or place (Cl. 1)

1 Safe berth KHARG ISLAND
Always afloat

</td><td colspan="2">

11. Discharging port or place (Cl. 1)

1 Safe berth Richards Bay always
afloat and/or 1 safe berth DURBAN
always afloat, rotation in Charterer's
option.

</td></tr>
<tr><td colspan="4">

12. Cargo (also state quantity and margin in Owners' option, if agreed; if full and complete cargo not agreed state "part cargo") (Cl. 1)

15,000 metric tons, 5% more or less in Owner's option, of sulphur in bulk

</td></tr>
<tr><td colspan="2">

13. Freight rate (also state if payable on delivered or intaken quantity) (Cl. 1)

9.85 US Dollars per metric ton less 1% in
lieu of weighing. 90% less commission to be
paid withing 8 working days. after advice has
been received of Bills of Lading signatures
but any way prior

</td><td colspan="2">

14. Freight payment (state currency and method of payment; also beneficiary and bank account) (Cl. 4)

Breaking bulk. Balance plus
demmurage or less despatch incurred
at ports of leading + discharging
to be paid after right and true
delivery of the cargo .*1

</td></tr>
<tr><td colspan="2">

15. Loading and discharging costs (state alternative (a) or (b) of Cl. 5; also indicate if vessel is gearless)

</td><td colspan="2">

16. Laytime (if separate laytime for load. and disch. is agreed, fill in a) and b). If total laytime for load. and disch., fill in c) only) (Cl. 6)

a) Laytime for loading

</td></tr>
<tr><td colspan="2" rowspan="2">

17. Shippers (state name and address) (Cl. 6)

Messrs. Abraham KIPPERS
Kharg Island, IRAN.

</td><td colspan="2">

b) Laytime for discharging

</td></tr>
<tr><td colspan="2">

c) Total laytime for loading and discharging
Cargo to be loaded & discharged by
Charterers' stevedores at *2

</td></tr>
<tr><td colspan="2">

18. Demurrage rate (loading and discharging) (Cl. 7)

US Dollars 3,050 - to be paid by Charters

</td><td colspan="2">

19. Cancelling date (Cl. 10)

20.2.52

</td></tr>
<tr><td colspan="4">

20. Brokerage commission and to whom payable (Cl. 14)

2.50% address commission due to Charterers and 2.50% to Messrs. ANGELS Ltd.

</td></tr>
<tr><td colspan="4">

21. Additional clauses covering special provisions, if agreed.

*1 within 10 days after receipt by Charterers of Owners' final freight account
supported by time sheets. full freight considered deemd earned on signing Bs/L and
non returnable ship and/or cargo lost or not lost. Freight to be paid in GENOA in US
dollars to Owners' Account with "A" Bank for the credit Messrs Aquarius Ltd., Account
No. 00023 m.v."ANAX". If a second discharging port is used, Charterers to pay an
extra of 0.50 US Dollars per metric ton on entire cargo.

*2 the average rate of 1,500 m.t. per weather working day of 24 consecutive hours
Fridays and Holidays exempted even if used.

</td></tr>
</table>

It is mutually agreed that this Contract shall be performed subject to the conditions contained in this Charter which shall include Part I as well as Part II. In the event of a conflict of conditions, the provisions of Part I shall prevail over those of Part II to the extent of such conflict.

<table>
<tr><td>

Signature (Owners)

For and on behalf of Owners

</td><td>

Signature (Charterers)

Messrs. Anonymous Ltd.

</td></tr>
</table>

PART II
"Gencon" Charter (As Revised 1922 and 1976)
Including "F.I.O." Alternative, etc.

last of the loading ports, if more than one, it appears that further 205
performance of the contract will subject the Vessel, her Master and 206
crew or her cargo, to war risks, the cargo shall be discharged, or if 207
the discharge has been commenced shall be completed, at any safe 208
port in vicinity of the port of discharge as may be ordered by the 209
Charterers. If no such orders shall be received from the Charterers 210
within 48 hours after the Owners have despatched a request by 211
telegram to the Charterers for the nomination of a substitute discharg- 212
ing port, the Owners shall be at liberty to discharge the cargo at 213
any safe port which they may, in their discretion, decide on and such 214
discharge shall be deemed to be due fulfilment of the contract of 215
affreightment. In the event of cargo being discharged at any such 216
other port, the Owners shall be entitled to freight as if the discharge 217
had been effected at the port or ports named in the Bill(s) of Lading 218
or to which the Vessel may have been ordered pursuant thereto. 219

(5) (a) The Vessel shall have liberty to comply with any directions 220
or recommendations as to loading, departure, arrival, routes, ports 221
of call, stoppages, destination, zones, waters, discharge, delivery or 222
in any other wise whatsoever (including any direction or recom- 223
mendation not to go to the port of destination or to delay proceeding 224
thereto or to proceed to some other port) given by any Government or 225
by any belligerent or by any organized body engaged in civil war, 226
hostilities or warlike operations or by any person or body acting or 227
purporting to act as or with the authority of any Government or 228
belligerent or of any such organized body or by any committee or 229
person having under the terms of the war risks insurance on the 230
Vessel, the right to give any such directions or recommendations. If, 231
by reason of or in compliance with any such direction or recom- 232
mendation, anything is done or is not done, such shall not be deemed 233
a deviation. 234

(b) If, by reason of or in compliance with any such directions or re- 235
commendations, the Vessel does not proceed to the port or ports 236
named in the Bill(s) of Lading or to which she may have been 237
ordered pursuant thereto, the Vessel may proceed to any port as 238
directed or recommended or to any safe port which the Owners in 239
their discretion may decide on and there discharge the cargo. Such 240
discharge shall be deemed to be due fulfilment of the contract of 241
affreightment and the Owners shall be entitled to freight as if 242
discharge had been effected at the port or ports named in the Bill(s) 243
of Lading or to which the Vessel may have been ordered pursuant 244
thereto. 245

(6) All extra expenses (including insurance costs) involved in discharg- 246
ing cargo at the loading port or in reaching or discharging the cargo 247
at any port as provided in Clauses 4 and 5 (b) hereof shall be paid 248
by the Charterers and/or cargo owners, and the Owners shall have 249
a lien on the cargo for all moneys due under these Clauses. 250

17. GENERAL ICE CLAUSE 251
Port of loading 252

(a) In the event of the loading port being inaccessible by reason of 253
ice when vessel is ready to proceed from her last port or at any 254
time during the voyage or on vessel's arrival or in case frost sets in 255
after vessel's arrival, the Captain for fear of being frozen in is at 256
liberty to leave without cargo, and this Charter shall be null and 257
void. 258

(b) If during loading the Captain, for fear of vessel being frozen in, 259
deems it advisable to leave, he has liberty to do so with what cargo 260
he has on board and to proceed to any other port or ports with 261
option of completing cargo for Owners' benefit for any port or ports 262
including port of discharge. Any part cargo thus loaded under this 263
Charter to be forwarded to destination at vessel's expense but 264
against payment of freight, provided that no extra expenses be 265
thereby caused to the Receivers, freight being paid on quantity 266
delivered (in proportion if lumpsum), all other conditions as per 267
Charter. 268

(c) In case of more than one loading port, and if one or more of 269
the ports are closed by ice, the Captain or Owners to be at liberty 270
either to load the part cargo at the open port and fill up elsewhere 271
for their own account as under section (b) or to declare the Charter 272
null and void unless Charterers agree to load full cargo at the open 273
port. 274

(d) This Ice Clause not to apply in the Spring. 275

Port of discharge 276

(a) Should ice (except in the Spring) prevent vessel from reaching 277
port of discharge Receivers shall have the option of keeping vessel 278
waiting until the re-opening of navigation and paying demurrage, or 279
of ordering the vessel to a safe and immediately accessible port 280
where she can safely discharge without risk of detention by ice. 281
Such orders to be given within 48 hours after Captain or Owners 282
have given notice to Charterers of the impossibility of reaching port 283
of destination. 284

(b) If during discharging the Captain for fear of vessel being frozen 285
in deems it advisable to leave, he has liberty to do so with what 286
cargo he has on board and to proceed to the nearest accessible 287
port where she can safely discharge. 288

(c) On delivery of the cargo at such port, all conditions of the Bill 289
of Lading shall apply and vessel shall receive the same freight as 290
if she had discharged at the original port of destination, except that if 291
the distance of the substituted port exceeds 100 nautical miles, the 292
freight on the cargo delivered at the substituted port to be increased 293
in proportion. 294

PART II
"Gencon" Charter (As Revised 1922 and 1976)
Including "F.I.O." Alternative, etc.

1. It is agreed between the party mentioned in Box 3 as Owners of the steamer or motor-vessel named in Box 5, of the gross/nett Register tons indicated in Box 6 and carrying about the number of tons of deadweight cargo stated in Box 7, now in position as stated in Box 8 and expected ready to load under this Charter about the date indicated in Box 9, and the party mentioned as Charterers in Box 4 that:
The said vessel shall proceed to the loading port or place stated in Box 10 ~~or so near thereto as she may safely get~~ and lie always afloat, and there load a full and complete cargo ~~(if shipment of deck cargo agreed same to be at Charterers' risk)~~ as stated in Box 12 (Charterers to provide all mats and/or wood for dunnage and any separations required, the Owners allowing the use of any dunnage wood on board if required) which the Charterers bind themselves to ship, and being so loaded the vessel shall proceed to the discharging port or place stated in Box 11 as ordered on signing Bills of Lading ~~or so near thereto as she may safely get and~~ lie always afloat and there deliver the cargo on being paid freight on ~~delivered or~~ intaken quantity as indicated in Box 13 at the rate stated in Box 13.

2. Owners' Responsibility Clause
[handwritten: *trimming to be under masters direction*]
Owners are to be responsible for loss of or damage to the goods or for delay in delivery of the goods only in case the loss, damage or delay has been caused by the improper or negligent stowage of the goods ~~(unless stowage performed by shippers/Charterers or their stevedores or servants)~~ or by personal want of due diligence on the part of the Owners or their Manager to make the vessel in all respects seaworthy and to secure that she is properly manned, equipped and supplied or by the personal act or default of the Owners or their Manager.
And the Owners are responsible for no loss or damage or delay arising from any other cause whatsoever, even from the neglect or default of the Captain or crew or some other person employed by the Owners on board or ashore for whose acts they would, but for this clause, be responsible, or from unseaworthiness of the vessel on loading or commencement of the voyage or at any time whatsoever. ~~Damage caused by contact with or leakage, smell or evaporation from other goods or by the inflammable or explosive nature or insufficient package of other goods not to be considered as caused by improper or negligent stowage, even if in fact so caused.~~

3. Deviation Clause
The vessel has liberty to call at any port or ports in any order, for any purpose, to sail without pilots, to tow and/or assist vessels in all situations, and also to deviate for the purpose of saving life and/or property.

4. Payment of Freight
The freight to be paid in the manner prescribed in Box 14 ~~in cash~~ without discount on delivery of the cargo at mean rate of ~~exchange~~ ruling on day or days of payment, the receivers of ~~the cargo being bound to pay freight on account during delivery, if required by~~ Captain or Owners.
~~Cash for vessel's ordinary disbursements at port of loading to be advanced by Charterers if required at highest current rate of exchange, subject to two per cent. to cover insurance and other expenses.~~

5. Loading/Discharging Costs
~~*(a) Gross Terms*~~
~~The cargo to be brought alongside in such a manner as to enable~~ vessel to take the goods with her own tackle. Charterers ~~to procure and pay the necessary men on shore or on board the lighters to do~~ the work there, vessel only heaving the cargo on board.
~~If the loading takes place by elevator, cargo to be put free in vessel's holds, Owners only paying trimming expenses.~~
~~Any pieces and/or packages of cargo over two tons weight, shall be loaded, stowed and discharged by Charterers at their risk and expense.~~
~~The cargo to be received by Merchants at their risk and expense alongside the vessel not beyond the reach of her tackle.~~

** (b) F.i.o. and free stowed/trimmed*
The cargo shall be brought into the holds, loaded, stowed and/or trimmed and taken from the holds and discharged by the Charterers or their Agents, free of any risk, liability and expense whatsoever to the Owners.
The Owners shall provide winches, motive power and winchmen from the Crew if requested and permitted; if not, the Charterers shall provide and pay for winchmen from shore and/or cranes, if any. (This provision shall not apply if vessel is gearless and stated as such in Box 15).
** indicate alternative (a) or (b), as agreed, in Box 15.*

6. Laytime
~~*(a) Separate laytime for loading and discharging*~~
~~The cargo shall be loaded within the number of running hours as~~ indicated in Box 16, weather permitting, Sundays and holidays excepted, unless used, in which event time actually used shall count.
The cargo shall be discharged within the number of running hours as indicated in Box 16, weather permitting, Sundays and holidays excepted, unless used, in which event time actually used shall count.
** (b) Total laytime for loading and discharging*
The cargo shall be loaded and discharged within the number of total running hours as indicated in Box 16, weather permitting, Sundays and holidays excepted, unless used, in which event time actually used shall count.
(c) Commencement of laytime (loading and discharging)
Laytime for loading and discharging shall commence at 1 p.m. if notice of readiness is given before noon, and at 6 a.m. next working day if notice given during office hours after noon. Notice at loading port to be given to the Shippers named in Box 17.
Time actually used before commencement of laytime shall count.
~~Time lost in waiting for berth to count as loading or discharging time, as the case may be.~~
** indicate alternative (a) or (b) as agreed, in Box 16.*

Demurrage
~~Ten running days on~~ demurrage at the rate stated in Box 18 per day or pro rata for any part of a day, ~~payable day by day, to be allowed Merchants altogether at ports of loading and discharging.~~

8. Lien Clause
Owners shall have a lien on the cargo for freight, dead-freight, demurrage ~~and damages for detention~~. Charterers shall remain responsible for dead-freight and demurrage ~~(including damages for detention)~~, incurred at port of loading. Charterers shall also remain responsible for freight and demurrage ~~(including damages for detention)~~ incurred at port of discharge, but only to such extent as the Owners have been unable to obtain payment thereof by exercising the lien on the cargo.

9. Bills of Lading
The Captain to sign Bills of Lading at such rate of freight as presented without prejudice to this Charterparty, but should the freight by Bills of Lading amount to less than the total chartered freight the difference to be paid to the Captain in cash on signing Bills of Lading.

10. Cancelling Clause [handwritten: *Lay days not to commence before 15/12/52.*]
Should the vessel not be ready to load (whether in berth or not) on or before the date indicated in Box 19, Charterers have the option of cancelling this contract, ~~such option to be declared, if demanded,~~ at least 48 hours before vessel's expected arrival ~~at port of loading.~~ ~~Should the vessel be delayed on account of average or otherwise, Charterers to be informed as soon as possible, and if the vessel is delayed for more than 10 days after the day she is stated to be expected ready to load, Charterers have the option of cancelling this contract, unless a cancelling date has been agreed upon.~~

11. General Average
General average to be settled according to York-Antwerp Rules, 1974. Proprietors of cargo to pay the cargo's share in the general expenses even if same have been necessitated through neglect or default of the Owners' servants (see clause 2).

12. Indemnity
Indemnity for non-performance of this Charterparty, proved damages, not exceeding estimated amount of freight.

13. Agency   [handwritten: *charterers* ... *their own*]
In every case the ~~Owners~~ shall appoint ~~his own Broker~~ or Agent [handwritten: *both*] at the port of loading and the port of discharge, [handwritten: *owners paying usual fees*]

14. Brokerage
A brokerage commission at the rate stated in Box 20 on the freight earned is due to the party mentioned in Box 20.
In case of non-execution at least ⅓ of the brokerage on the estimated amount of freight and dead-freight to be paid by the Owners to the Brokers as indemnity for the latter's expenses and work. In case of more voyages the amount of indemnity to be mutually agreed.

15. GENERAL STRIKE CLAUSE
Neither Charterers nor Owners shall be responsible for the consequences of any strikes or lock-outs preventing or delaying the fulfilment of any obligations under this contract.
If there is a strike or lock-out affecting the loading of the cargo, or any part of it, when vessel is ready to proceed from her last port or at any time during the voyage to the port or ports of loading or after her arrival there, Captain or Owners may ask Charterers to declare, that they agree to reckon the laydays as if there were no strike or lock-out. Unless Charterers have given such declaration in writing (by telegram, if necessary) within 24 hours, Owners shall have the option of cancelling this contract. If part cargo has already been loaded, Owners must proceed with same, (freight payable on loaded quantity only) having liberty to complete with other cargo on the way for their own account.
If there is a strike or lock-out affecting the discharge of the cargo on or after vessel's arrival at or off port of discharge and same has not been settled within 48 hours, Receivers shall have the option of keeping vessel waiting until such strike or lock-out is at an end against paying half demurrage after expiration of the time provided for discharging, or of ordering the vessel to a safe port where she can safely discharge without risk of being detained by strike or lock-out. Such orders to be given within 48 hours after Captain or Owners have given notice to Charterers of the strike or lock-out affecting the discharge. On delivery of the cargo at such port, all conditions of this Charterparty and of the Bill of Lading shall apply and vessel shall receive the same freight as if she had discharged at the original port of destination, except that if the distance of the substituted port exceeds 100 nautical miles, the freight on the cargo delivered at the substituted port to be increased in proportion.

16. War Risks ("Voywar 1950")
(1) In these clauses "War Risks" shall include any blockade or any action which is announced as a blockade by any Government or by any belligerent or by any organized body, sabotage, piracy, and any actual or threatened war, hostilities, warlike operations, civil war, civil commotion, or revolution.
(2) If at any time before the Vessel commences loading, it appears that performance of the contract will subject the Vessel or her Master and crew or her cargo to war risks at any stage of the adventure, the Owners shall be entitled by letter or telegram despatched to the Charterers, to cancel this Charter.
(3) The Master shall not be required to load cargo or to continue loading or to proceed on or to sign Bill(s) of Lading for any adventure on which or any port at which it appears that the Vessel, her Master and crew or her cargo will be subjected to war risks. In the event of the exercise by the Master of his right under this Clause after part or full cargo has been loaded, the Master shall be at liberty either to discharge such cargo at the loading port or to proceed therewith. In the latter case the Vessel shall have liberty to carry other cargo for Owners' benefit and accordingly to proceed to and load or discharge such other cargo at any other port or ports whatsoever, backwards or forwards, although in a contrary direction to or out of or beyond the ordinary route. In the event of the Master electing to proceed with part cargo under this Clause freight shall in any case be payable on the quantity delivered.
(4) If at the time the Master elects to proceed with part or full cargo under Clause 3, or after the Vessel has left the loading port, or the

AUTO-INTER CONTROL LTD.
7, ANONYMOUS STREET, ANTWERP

Certificate of Supervision No. Ro 2-440427

Orderer:

Sellers:

Buyers: SIX, SEVEN Agencies Ltd.

Commodity: "French white crystal" sugar of Dutch origin
                           complying with the requirements of Dutch
                           10/1958 packed in polythene bags of 25 Kgs.
                           nett each.
Contract No:
                           1212/3535

Letter of Credit: No. 4567 - 008930

Quantity acc.
to B/L No.1:   25,000 Kgs.

Port of Loading: ANTWERP

Vessel: "ANAX"

Timesheet: Beginning of loading: 10/10/80   10.00 Hrs
                           Completed loading: 10/10/80   14.00 Hrs

Results of Supervision:

1. Quality: The quality corresponds to French white crystal
                           sugar and according to DIN 1164 which corresponds
                           to Dut. 12/1958

2. Inspection of packing: The merchandise is packed in single polythene bags

3. Quantity: According to the B/L 25,000 Kgs were loaded on the
                           m.v. "ANAX"

                           ANTWERP 12/10/80

We exlusively work according to the "General Terms for the
Supervision of Goods" The findings do not exempt suppliers
from their contractual obligations. Rights of recourse cannot
be claimed toward "Atuo-Inter Control Ltd." on the basis of
findings contained in this document of supervision.

1.Shipper: ONE,TWO Shipping Co. Ltd.

5.Number
  of Invoice: 1234

  No. of
  buyer's order   Date: 12/10/80

  Import Licence   valid until:

2.Receiver:

6.Buyer:
  SIX, SEVEN Agencies

  Agent:

3.Auxillary address:

7.Pricing/
  Basis of delivery: F.O.B. ANTWERPEN
  Terms   STOWED
  of payment: Irrevocable Credit
                     No:4567 - 008930

4.Delivered by: Date of shipment:
  SHIP   LO/1O/8O

                         Delivery station:

Name of the ship: Shipping port: Date of payment:
   m.v. "ANAX"   ANTWERPEN

Port of destination: Destination(station):

   LAGOS, Nigeria

8.Marks and No.   Cases/Number and kind   Quantity   Price
                         Commodity   Unit of measure per unit   total

---

   1000 Bags   "French white crystal" sugar of Dutch origin
                        complying with the requirements of DUT.1O/1958,
   ABC 3333   packed in polythene bags of 25 Kgs. nett each.
   LAGOS

9. Cases(Dimensions)

       1000 Polythene bags of
       sugar - 25,000 Kgs.

Weight gross:	Volume m3:
25,000Kgs net:	

10. Manufacturer/   The Chamber of Foreign Trade of the Netherlands
    Foreign trade enterprise: certifies that according to the presented
                           documents and to the authentic affirmation given to this
                           effect, the goods mentioned in the above specification
       "Granulated Dutch   have been produced in the Netherlands.
       Associates"

                           place and date:
                           12.10.80 Brussels

                                signature

COPY ONLY

**CLAIMS PAYABLE IN
LONDON**

LLOYD'S

Exporters
Reference

**THIS CERTIFICATE
REQUIRES ENDORSEMENT**

Certificate of Insurance No. C 000/

This is to Certify that there has been deposited with the Committee of Lloyd's an Open Cover effected by *J. O. B. Long & Co., Ltd.,* of Lloyd's, acting on behalf of *The Herne Bay Supply Company* with Underwriters at Lloyd's, dated the *First* day of *January, 1978,* and that the said Underwriters have undertaken to issue to *J. O. B. Long & Co., Ltd.* Policy/Policies of Marine Insurance at Lloyd's to cover, up to *£10,000 (or equivalent in other currencies)* in all by any one steamer *or sending by air and/or parcel post, Golf Equipment, other interests held covered* to be shipped on or before the *Thirty-first* day of *December, 1980,* from any port or ports, place or places in *the United Kingdom* to any port or ports, place or places in *the World;* and that *The Herne Bay Supply Company* are entitled to declare against the said Open Cover the shipments attaching thereto.

This document being a copy is unsigned, but the original Certificate and the duplicate thereof is here signed on behalf of the Committee of Lloyd's.

Dated at Lloyd's, London, 2nd October, 1978.

Conveyance	From	
Via/To	To	INSURED VALUE/Currency:

Marks and Numbers	Interest

We hereby declare for Insurance under the said Cover interest as specified above so valued subject to the terms of the Standard Form of Lloyd's Marine Policy and to the special conditions stated below and on the back hereof.

Institute Cargo Clauses (All Risks) (1.1.63) excluding rust, oxidisation, discoloration, twisting and bending.
Subject to Institute Replacement (Clause (1.1.34).
Institute War Clauses (1.7.76) or Institute War Clauses (including on-carriage by Air) (1.7.76) or Institute War Clauses (Air) (excluding sendings by Post) (1.1.71) or Institute War Clauses for the insurance of sendings by Post (1.1.71) as applicable.
Institute Strikes Riots and Civil Commotions Clauses (1.1.63).

Underwriters agree losses, if any, shall be payable to the order of HERNE BAY SUPPLY COMPANY on surrender of this Certificate.

In the event of loss or damage which may result in a claim under this Insurance, immediate notice should be given to the Lloyd's Agent at the port or place where the loss or damage is discovered in order that he may examine the goods and issue a survey report.

(Survey fee is customarily paid by claimant and included in valid claim against Underwriters.)

In the event of claim all documents, including this Certificate and survey report, to be sent to the Brokers stated below:—

This Certificate not valid unless the Declaration be signed by

THE HERNE BAY SUPPLY COMPANY.

Dated at Herne Bay,

Signed

Brokers: J. O. B. Long & Co., Ltd.,
999, Lloyd's Street, Insurance Avenue, London, E.C.0.

12567/9

"The Institute Clauses printed or referred to herein are those current at the date of printing of this Certificate but where such Clauses are subsequently revised then the revised Institute Clauses shall apply if this insurance attaches on or after the date of the revised Clauses."

<table>
<tr><td>

DOCUMENTATION OF CLAIMS

To enable claims to be dealt with promptly, the Assured or their Agents are advised to submit all available supporting documents without delay, including when applicable:—

1. Original policy or certificate of insurance.
2. Original or copy shipping invoices, together with shipping specification and/or weight notes.
3. Original Bill of Lading and/or other contract of carriage.
4. Survey report or other documentary evidence to show the extent of the loss or damage.
5. Landing account and weight notes at final destination.
6. Correspondence exchanged with the Carriers and other Parties regarding their liability for the loss or damage.

</td><td>

IMPORTANT
LIABILITY OF CARRIERS, BAILEES OR OTHER THIRD PARTIES

It is the duty of the Assured and their Agents, in all cases, to take such measures as may be reasonable for the purpose of averting or minimising a loss and to ensure that all rights against Carriers, Bailees or other third parties are properly preserved and exercised. In particular, the Assured or their Agents are required:—

1. To claim immediately on the Carriers, Port Authorities or other Bailees for any missing packages.
2. In no circumstances, except under written protest, to give clean receipts where goods are in doubtful condition.
3. When delivery is made by Container, to ensure that the Container and its seals are examined immediately by their responsible official. If the Container is delivered damaged or with seals broken or missing or with seals other than as stated in the shipping documents, to clause the delivery receipt accordingly and retain all defective or irregular seals for subsequent identification.
4. To apply immediately for survey by Carriers' or other Bailees' Representatives if any loss or damage be apparent and claim on the Carriers or other Bailees for any actual loss or damage found at such survey.
5. To give notice in writing to the Carriers or other Bailees within 3 days of delivery if the loss or damage was not apparent at the time of taking delivery.

Note.—The Consignees or their Agents are recommended to make themselves familiar with the Regulations of the Port Authorities at the port of discharge.

</td></tr>
</table>

NOTE.—It is necessary for the Assured when they become aware of an event which is "held covered" under this insurance to give prompt notice to Underwriters and the right to such cover is dependent upon compliance with this obligation.

Appendix C

Convention on the Territorial Sea and the Contiguous Zone

(Text as adopted by the Conference at its 20th plenary meeting)

The States Parties to this Convention

Have agreed as follows:–

PART I

TERRITORIAL SEA

Section I.—General

ARTICLE 1

1. The sovereignty of a State extends, beyond its land territory and its internal waters, to a belt of sea to its coast, described as the territorial sea.

2. This sovereignty is exercised subject to the provisions of these articles and to other rules of international law.

ARTICLE 2

The sovereignty of a coastal State extends to the air space over the territorial sea as well as to its bed and subsoil.

Section II.—Limits of the territorial sea

ARTICLE 3

Except where otherwise provided in these articles, the normal baseline for measuring the breadth of the territorial sea is the low-water line along the coast as marked on large-scale charts officially recognised by the coastal State.

ARTICLE 4

1. In localities where the coast line is deeply indented and cut into, or if there is a fringe of islands along the coast in its immediate vicinity, the method of straight baselines joining appropriate points may be employed in drawing the baseline from which the breadth of the territorial sea is measured.

2. The drawing of such baselines must not depart to any appreciable extent from the general direction of the coast, and the sea areas lying within the lines must be sufficiently closely linked to the land domain to be subject to the régime of internal waters.

3. Baselines shall not be drawn to and from low-tide elevations, unless lighthouses or similar installations which are permanently above sea level have been built on them.

4. Where the method of straight baselines is applicable under the provisions of paragraph 1, account may be taken, in determining particular baselines, of economic interests peculiar to the region concerned, the reality and the importance of which are clearly evidenced by a long usage.

5. The system of straight baselines may not be applied by a State in such a manner as to cut off from the high seas the territorial sea of another State.

6. The coastal State must clearly indicate straight baselines on charts, to which due publicity must be given.

ARTICLE 5

1. Waters on the landward side of the baseline of the territorial sea form part of the internal waters of the State.

2. Where the establishment of a straight baseline in accordance with article 4 has the effect of enclosing as internal waters areas which previously had been considered as part of the territorial sea or of the high seas, a right of innocent passage, as provided in articles 14 to 23, shall exist in those waters.

ARTICLE 6

The outer limit of the territorial sea is the line every point of which is at a distance from the nearest point of the baseline equal to the breadth of the territorial sea.

ARTICLE 7

1. This article relates only to bays the coasts of which belong to a single State.

2. For the purposes of these articles, a bay is a well-marked indentation whose penetration is in such proportion to the width of its mouth as to contain landlocked waters and constitute more than a mere curvature of the coast. An indentation shall not, however, be regarded as a bay unless its area is as large as, or larger than, that of the semi-circle whose diameter is a line drawn across the mouth of that indentation.

3. For the purpose of measurement, the area of an indentation is that lying between the low-water mark around the shore of the indentation and a line joining the low-water marks of its natural entrance points. Where because of the presence of islands, an indentation has more than one mouth, the semi-circle shall be drawn on a line as long as the sum total of the lengths of the lines across the different mouths. Islands within an indentation shall be included as if they were part of the water area of the indentation.

4. If the distance between the low-water marks of the natural entrance points of a bay does not exceed twenty-four miles, a closing line may be drawn between these two low-water marks, and the waters enclosed thereby shall be considered as internal waters.

5. Where the distance between the low-water marks of the natural entrance points of a bay exceeds twenty-four miles, a straight baseline of twenty-four miles shall be drawn within the bay in such a manner as to enclose the maximum area of water that is possible with a line of that length.

6. The foregoing provisions shall not apply to so-called "historic" bays, or in any case where the straight baseline system provided for in article 4 is applied.

ARTICLE 8

For the purpose of delimiting the territorial sea, the outermost permanent harbour works which form an integral part of the harbour system shall be regarded as forming part of the coast.

ARTICLE 9

Roadsteads which are normally used for the loading, unloading and anchoring of ships, and which would otherwise be situated wholly or partly outside the outer limit of the territorial sea, are included in the territorial sea. The coastal State must clearly demarcate such roadsteads and indicate them on charts together with their boundaries to which due publicity must be given.

ARTICLE 10

1. An island is a naturally-formed area of land, surrounded by water, which is above water at high tide.

2. The territorial sea of an island is measured in accordance with the provisions of these articles.

ARTICLE 11

1. A low-tide elevation is a naturally-formed area of land which is surrounded by and above water at low-tide but submerged at high tide. Where a low-tide elevation is situated wholly or partly at a distance not exceeding the breadth of the territorial sea from the mainland or an island, the low-water line on that elevation may be used as the baseline for measuring the breadth of the territorial sea.

2. Where a low-tide elevation is wholly situated at a distance exceeding the breadth of the territorial sea from the mainland or an island, it has no territorial sea of its own.

ARTICLE 12

1. Where the coasts of two States are opposite or adjacent to each other, neither of the two States is entitled, failing agreement between them to the contrary, to extend its territorial sea beyond the median line every point of which is equidistant from the nearest points on the baselines from which the breadth of the territorial seas of each of the two States is measured. The provisions of this paragraph shall not apply, however, where it is necessary by reason of historic title or other special circumstances to delimit the territorial seas of the two States in a way which is at variance with this provision.

2. The line of delimitation between the territorial seas of two States lying opposite to each other or adjacent to each other shall be marked on large-scale charts officially recognised by the coastal States.

ARTICLE 13

If a river flows directly into the sea, the baseline shall be a straight line across the mouth of the river between points on the low-tide line of its banks.

Section III.—Right of innocent passage

Sub-section A.—Rules applicable to all ships

ARTICLE 14

1. Subject to the provisions of these articles, ships of all States whether coastal or not, shall enjoy the right of innocent passage through the territorial sea.

2. Passage means navigation through the territorial sea for the purpose either of traversing that sea without entering internal waters, or of proceeding to internal waters, or of making for the high seas from internal waters.

3. Passage includes stopping and anchoring, but only in so far as the same are incidental to ordinary navigation or are rendered necessary by *force majeure* or by distress.

4. Passage is innocent so long as it is not prejudicial to the peace, good order or security of the coastal State. Such passage shall take place in conformity with these articles and with other rules of international law.

5. Passage of foreign fishing vessels shall not be considered innocent if they do not observe such laws and regulations as the coastal State may make and publish in order to prevent these vessels from fishing in the territorial sea.

6. Submarines are required to navigate on the surface and to show their flag.

ARTICLE 15

1. The coastal State must not hamper innocent passage through the territorial sea.

2. The coastal State is required to give appropriate publicity to any dangers to navigation, of which it has knowledge, within its territorial sea.

ARTICLE 16

1. The coastal State may take the necessary steps in its territorial sea to prevent passage which is not innocent.

2. In the case of ships proceeding to internal waters, the coastal State shall also have the right to take the necessary steps to prevent any breach of the conditions to which admission of those ships to those waters is subject.

3. Subject to the provisions of paragraph 4, the coastal State may, without discrimination amongst foreign ships, suspend temporarily in specified areas of its territorial sea the innocent passage of foreign ships if such suspension is essential for the protection of its security. Such suspension shall take effect only after having been duly published.

4. There shall be no suspension of the innocent passage of foreign ships through straits which are used for international navigation between one part of the high seas and another part of the high seas or the territorial sea of a foreign State.

ARTICLE 17

Foreign ships exercising the right of innocent passage shall comply with the laws and regulations enacted by the coastal State in conformity with these articles and other rules of international law and, in particular, with such laws and regulations relating to transport and navigation.

Sub-section B.—Rules applicable to merchant ships

ARTICLE 18

1. No charge may be levied upon foreign ships by reason only of their passage through the territorial sea.

2. Charges may be levied upon a foreign ship passing through the territorial sea as payment only for specific services rendered to the ship. These charges shall be levied without discrimination.

ARTICLE 19

1. The criminal jurisdiction of the coastal State should not be exercised on board a foreign ship passing through the territorial sea to arrest any person or to conduct any investigation in connexion with any crime committed on board the ship during its passage, save only in the following cases:

> (a) If the consequences of the crime extend to the coastal State; or

(*b*) If the crime is of a kind to disturb the peace of the
       country or the good order of the territorial sea; or
(*c*) If the assistance of the local authorities has been
       requested by the captain of the ship or by the consul of
       the country whose flag the ship flies; or
(*d*) If it is necessary for the suppression of illicit traffic in
       narcotic drugs.

2. The above provisions do not affect the right of the coastal State
to take any steps authorised by its laws for the purpose of an arrest or
investigation on board a foreign ship passing through the territorial
sea after leaving internal waters.

3. In the cases provided for in paragraphs 1 and 2 of this article,
the coastal State shall, if the captain so requests, advise the consular
authority of the flag State before taking any steps, and shall facilitate
contact between such authority and the ship's crew. In cases of
emergency this notification may be communicated while the
measures are being taken.

4. In considering whether or how an arrest should be made, the
local authorities shall pay due regard to the interests of navigation.

5. The coastal State may not take any steps on board a foreign ship
passing through the territorial sea to arrest any person or to conduct
any investigation in connexion with any crime committed before the
ship entered the territorial sea, if the ship, proceeding from a foreign
port, is only passing through the territorial sea without entering
internal waters.

Article 20

1. The coastal State should not stop or divert a foreign ship passing
through the territorial sea for the purpose of exercising civil jurisdiction in relation to a person on board the ship.

2. The coastal State may not levy execution against or arrest the
ship for the purpose of any civil proceedings, save ony in respect of
obligations or liabilities assumed or incurred by the ship itself in the
course or for the purpose of its voyage through the waters or the
coastal State.

3. The provision of the previous paragraph are without prejudice
to the right of the coastal State, in accordance with its laws, to levy
execution against or to arrest, for the purpose of any civil proceedings, a foreign ship lying in the territorial sea, or passing through the
territorial sea after leaving internal waters.

Sub-section C.—Rules applicable to government ships other than warships

ARTICLE 21

The rules contained in sub-sections A and B shall also apply to government ships operated for commercial purposes.

ARTICLE 22

1. The rules contained in sub-section A and in article 18 shall apply to government ships operated for non-commercial purposes.

2. With such exceptions as are contained in the provisions referred to in the preceding paragraph, nothing in these articles affects the immunities which such ships enjoy under these articles or other rules of international law.

Sub-section D.—Rule applicable to warships

ARTICLE 23

If any warship does not comply with the regulations of the coastal State concerning passage through the territorial sea and disregards any request for compliance which is made to it, the coastal State may require the warship to leave the territorial sea.

PART II

CONTIGUOUS ZONE

ARTICLE 24

1. In a zone of the high seas contiguous to its territorial sea, the coastal State may exercise the control necessary to:

    (*a*) Prevent infringement of its customs, fiscal, immigration or sanitary regulations within its territory or territorial sea;

    (*b*) Punish infringement of the above regulations committed within its territory or territorial sea.

2. The contiguous zone may not extend beyond twelve miles from the baseline from which the breadth of the territorial sea is measured.

3. Where the coasts of two States are opposite or adjacent to each other, neither of the two States is entitled, failing agreement between them to the contrary, to extend its contiguous zone beyond the median line every point of which is equidistant from the nearest points on the baselines from which the breadth of the territorial seas of the two States is measured.

PART III

FINAL ARTICLES

ARTICLE 25

The provisions of this Convention shall not affect conventions or other international agreements already in force, as between States Parties to them.

ARTICLE 26

This Convention shall, until 31 October 1958, be open for signature by all States Members of the United Nations or of any of the specialized agencies and by any other State invited by the General Assembly of the United Nations to become a Party to the Convention.

ARTICLE 27

This Convention is subject to ratification. The instruments of ratification shall be deposited with the Secretary-General of the United Nations.

ARTICLE 28

This Convention shall be opened for accession by any States belonging to any of the categories mentioned in article 26. The instrument of accession shall be deposited with the Secretary-General of the United Nations.

Appendix D

PROTECTION AGAINST SHIPPING AND CARGO FRAUD

CONFERENCE—HONG KONG—25/4/80

CLASSIFICATION SOCIETIES

Their Role: Advantages and Disadvantages of strict compliance with their Rules

by

R. A. POWELL

In the context of trying to ascertain the role of Classification Societies in protecting against shipping frauds, it is important to appreciate what are the objectives of the Classification Society. Of course, Classification by definition is no more than a systematic arrangement into class. So far so good. But why classification of ships?

In the first quarter of the last century an immense number of maritime disasters took place. For example, during the winter of 1821/1822 approximately 2,000 vessels were sunk with the loss of thousands of lives in the North Sea alone. That almost sounds like a misplaced excerpt from the introduction to the Far East Regional Investigation Team's Report; there is nevertheless a real analogy to be drawn between those sinkings and the spate of recent losses which have given such cause for concern as to justify wide publicity and, of course, this conference. History does repeat itself, and once the insurance market is faced with tremendous losses for whatever reason, it will attempt to analyse the cause of loss and will seek to remedy the situation. The result of the winter of 1821/22 was the bankruptcy of many insurance companies, and the realisation of those that survived that they had been taking unreasonable risks because they had little or no information about the condition of vessels they were insuring, or in which their insured cargo was carried. In fact, they had been taking unknown risks to the point where one could even imagine a defence founded upon the unenforceability of wagering contracts. However, the resistant core of the early 19th Century marine insurance market bore fruit, there blossomed forth the Classification Society, firstly in the form of the predecessor to Bureau Veritas in 1828, and almost before B.V. had taken root it was hotly pursued by Lloyd's Register Classification Society in 1834. To forestall criticism, I hasten to point out that Lloyds maintained a Register of Ships from about 1764 and there was thus no doubt some element of "classification" but not classification in the subsequently recognised sense. According to the notice announcing the establishment of the earlier of those Societies, its aims were:

> "To acquaint the underwriters with the qualities and defects of the vessels frequenting the harbours of the United Kingdom and of the Netherlands (including Holland and Belgium), to be useful:
> — to the underwriters, by keeping them off bad ships,
> — to the owners, who maintain correctly their vessels, by drawing to them the charters,
> — to the business world, by pointing out the vessels which are fit to carry its goods,
> — to humanity by contributing to reduce the credit and the number of vessels who expose their crews to sea disasters."

You will note that as in any commercial approach to shipping, the safety of life at sea came last.

The aims of Classification Societies thus defined have not changed since. The object is still to supply information about the reliability of merchant vessels, but the Societies' role has enlarged and they are now an inherent part of the process of designing building and operating merchant vessels, and it is every credit to the Classification Societies that the shipping community transcending as it does international barriers places its reliance upon the concept of classed ships, that is vessels designed built and maintained to engineering standards established and administered by Classification Societies.

It is not my task today to take you through the minutiae of Classification requirements or to compare the Rules of one Society with another, or to deal with the differences between exclusive and non-exclusive Class Surveyors. It is sufficient for me to say that I believe that a vessel fully classed and class maintained with an established and reputable Classification Society should, in theory, be able to face and withstand ordinary dangers inherent in carrying cargo from one port to another. But unfortunately theory is not enough and this has been appreciated by the P. & I. Clubs who require Condition Surveys to be carried out annually on overage tonnage, and yet despite all these surveys ships still sink and ships go to sea in a very unseaworthy state. In one recent case, having had her deck perfunctorily surveyed by a Classification Society surveyor in South Africa, resulting in class being maintained for her voyage to Japan, a vessel arrived in Hong Kong with no less than 67 corrosion holes in her coamings and weather deck through which naturally enough seawater poured onto the cargo despite the crew's valiant attempts to plug the holes with innumerable wooden wedges. In another recent example of a fully classed and class maintained vessel, a technical expert who was walking across the deck of a vessel, on which I had asked him to attend, put his foot through the deck up to his knee. Fortunately, he was not hurt. Then there was the case of a mature 22 year old vessel, naturally fully classed and class maintained, and having passed appropriate Condition Surveys, that sank with a full cargo—though no loss of life—in the circumstances where she had not seen the inside of a drydock for more than $2\frac{1}{2}$ years, and where in the knowledge that she had grounded and suffered bottom damage, the Classification Society had granted at the Owners' request no less than 4 extensions of drydocking survey. If the Society's Rules had been applied strictly, or even reasonably, that loss would not have occurred. I do not consider blame attaches to the shipowner who applying understandable commercial criteria wanted to delay incurring the cost of drydocking. When interviewing the Chief Officer of another vessel not very long ago, trying to find out why his vessel sank with its cargo, he readily admitted that the bulkheads between the vessel's holds were in such a state of advanced corrosion that the application of a chipping hammer was something to be avoided. Those bulkheads due to their age and, in my opinion, inefficient and inadequate survey had no water-tight integrity.

These are but few of the hundreds of frightening examples of the condition of vessels afloat today fully classed and class maintained, and possessing (although not in every case) current P. & I. Condition Surveys. One may ask what went wrong and what continues to go wrong? I am not critical of the Rules of Classification Societies—except perhaps insofar as there may be different standards for National Flag carriers and foreign vessels—but I am critical of the apparent unwillingness or inability of those concerned to apply the Rules in such a way as to achieve their objective. You may ask whether this is an appropriate topic when considering protection against shipping fraud rather than general cargo liabilities. I think it is appropriate because out of the many vessels that have been lost in circumstances where those investigating the losses have necessarily had to carefully examine the possibility of fraud, there are very very few vessels less than 10 years old, and the vast majority are much older. Indeed, it can almost be safely assumed that the stock-in-trade of the scuttler or would-be scuttler is a "rust-bucket." I accept that if he didn't have a "rust-bucket" but had a modern expensive vessel there is still the possibility that he would try to defraud his hull underwriter, or arrange such a high value cargo fraud that he need not concern himself with the recovery of the value of his vessel, but whilst there may be exceptions the would-be scuttler is much more likely to gamble with lower stakes. I am not advocating that every vessel over 10 or 15 years old should automatically be scrapped, or that the Rules be applied with such unreasonably vigour that to operate any venerable vessel would be economic suicide, but I am saying that with reasonably strict compliance with the Rules laid down by reputable Classification Societies, the number of "rust-buckets" will be reduced and they will hopefully and eventually become things of the past, and with their passing there will be an automatic reduction in the volume of maritime fraud.

Why then is it that there is, at present, a gap between the theory and the practice? I am quite certain that the vast majority of Classification Society surveyors are more than adequately qualified and rightly enjoy the reputation of absolute integrity and impartiality, but I am not blind to the many occasions when it has been suggested to me during the course of my career and, particularly in the last 2 or 3 years, that a financial inducement in the right hands, in the right place, and at the right time will produce appropriate Classification Society Certificates. Indeed, I believe it is not unknown for Certificates to be issued without even an attendance by the Surveyor on board the vessel! Fortunately it is not for me to consider whether it is even possible that such things might or even could happen, but if it is possible there should be a concerted effort by all Classification Societies to eradicate by whatever means there are available the very situations in which corruption might or could occur. It may cost money to do it but the cost would be insignificant and, in any event, would in due course be off-set so far as the ultimate consumer is concerned by lower insurance premia. Spot checks by roving special inspectors might be one answer. In other words the Classification Societies have assumed a policing role and I am suggesting that they should be seen to operate a self-policing system. It might be unpopular but the Societies must jealously guard their reputations and must be seen to be beyond reproach. They have the power of veto—they can withdraw class—and they must exercise that power whenever it is necessary so to do.

Statistics are something I abhor because although in themselves, depending upon their source, they may be factual it is what is deduced from statistics that is so often misleading or even inaccurate. Nevertheless, it is noteworthy, though not surprising, that the Far

East Regional Investigation Team[1] found that more than 50 per cent. of the 48 total losses they investigated happened to be classed with one particular Classification Society, and I would add, for good measure, about 85 per cent. sailed under the Panamanian flag.

There is no doubt that there is very hard competition between the Classification Societies for work; competition can in some circumstances improve standards, but unless it is carefully monitored it might, in other circumstances, prove to be a contributing factor in the general lowering of standards. The industry should be looking for the highest attainable quality control and not cut-price classification.

Fortunately, in many parts of the world there are conferences and discussion groups seeking to find the elusive answer to the question of how to prevent shipping fraud. There is no magic wand that I can wave that would produce the answer, but I believe an answer is to be found when you look at that bad winter in 1821, and find that standards of inspection having consequentially improved those catastrophic losses were not repeated. In the last 2 or 3 years there have been an incredible number of total losses (not all of which were in suspicious circumstances), and I would suggest that strict compliance with Classification Society Rules would be one way to minimise or prevent similar losses in the future. The role of the Classification Society is antagonistic. They should concern themselves with safety and safety alone, whereas shipowners particularly of over-age vessels strive to limit the funds they spend on the maintenance of their vessels. The policing role of the Classification Society must not be compromised. Whatever the cost strict compliance with their Rules can only result in the saving of lives and ships and their cargoes, and would thus greatly benefit the industry as a whole.

[1] The F.E.R.I.T. investigation

Appendix E

Ship Registration

Many maritime nations have a system of registration of vessels sailing under their own national flag whilst others register vessels of many other nations as well. The following is a list of the principle societies or bureaux:

AB	American Bureau of Shipping, Classification Soc.
BV	Bureau Veritas France.
DSRK	Deutsche Schiffs Revision and Klassifikation.
GL	Germanisher Lloyd.
H.R.	Hellenic Register of Shipping.
J.R.	Jugaslav Register.
L.R.	Lloyds Register.
N.K.	Nippon Kyokai.
N.V.	Norske Veritas.
P.R.	Polish Register.
R.I.	Registro Italiano.

Glossary of Terms

Ad Valorem	According to value, *i.e.* a freight rate calculated upon the cargo value rather than on volume or other dimension.
B/L	Bill of Lading.
BSC	British Shippers Council.
C & F	Cost and Freight.
C.I.F.	Cost Insurance Freight.
C.I.F. & E.	Cost Insurance Freight, with an additional clause covering exchange variation.
C.I.M.	International convention on carriage of goods by rail.
C.O.D.	Cash on delivery, or customer's own delivery.
C.T.O.	Combined, or through transport operator.
C.W.E.	Cleared without examination.
Dead freight	Space booked on board ship but not used.
Demurrage	Money paid for delay beyond contractual loading/unloading dates.

ETA	Estimated time of arrival.
ETD	Estimated time of departure.
Ex Works	A price quoted Ex Works is a price charged to a buyer collecting from seller's premises.
F.O.B.	Free on board.
F.P.A.	Free of particular average. An insurance term.
G.A.	General Average. An insurance term.
G.C.B.S.	General Council of British Shipping.
G.R.T.	Gross Registered Tons.
Hague Rules	1924 International Convention on Carriage of Goods by Sea.
I.C.C.	International Chamber of Commerce.
I.L.O.	International Labour Organisation.
IMCO	Inter-Governmental Maritime Consultative Organisation.
INCOTERMS	Standard terms for international trade compiled and published by the I.C.C., *i.e.* C.I.F., F.O.B., etc.
I.T.F.	International Transport Worker's Federation.
MANIFEST	Inventory of cargo loaded aboard.
Mate's receipt	Certificate of goods loaded from which B/L is prepared.
N.R.T.	Net registered tons.
O.E.C.D.	Organisation for Economic Co-operation & Development.
P & I Club	Protection and Indemnity Association.
Poincare Franc	National gold franc whose value is variable with inflation and currency changes. Used as an international unit of liability calculation.
T.C.	Time charter.
T.I.R.	Transport International Routier.
U.L.C.C.	Ultra large crude carrier (supertanker).
U.N.C.T.A.D.	United Nations Conference on Trade and Development.
V.A.T.	Value Added Tax—corresponds with the French T.V.A. and similar EEC taxes.
V.L.C.C.	Very large crude carrier.

Bibliography

Constitutional and Administrative Law by S. A. de Smith (Penguin).
   EEC Shipping Policy: *Flags of Convenience* (Economic & Social
   Committee of the European Communities, 1979).
Elements of Shipping by Allan E. Branch (Chapman & Hall, 4th ed.,
   1977).
Everyman's United Nations (Office of Public Information, UN Publica-
   tions E.67-1-5). A handbook of the UN during its first 20 years.
International Law by Malcolm Shaw (Heddse Stoughton, 1977).
International Court of Justice Year Books 1978–1979.
Flags of Convenience (I.T.F. Pamphlet).
Law and International Trade (Athenanm Verlag, Frankfurt, 1973).
"Ships Flying Flags of Convenience" by Professor Jnr. dr. Folke
   Schmidt, University of Stockholm (Offprint from *Journal of
   Maritime Law,* Vol 12, Oslo, 1972).
"Under which Flag" by Charles H. Blyth (a paper read to the
   Honourable Company of Master Mariners, London, 1975).

Appendix F

SECOND INTERNATIONAL SEMINAR

ON THE PREVENTION OF SHIPPING FRAUD

(Waldorf Astoria, New York)

"PROTECTION UNDER THE COMMON LAW AGAINST FRAUD AND MISREPRESENTATION"

Paper presented by

THE LORD HACKING

Partner, Lane & Partners, London

Thursday, 26th June, 1980

A. Introduction

One of the oldest statutes upon which reliance is still placed in England, the United States of America and countries in the British Commonwealth is the *Statute of Frauds*. It was enacted by Parliament sitting in Westminster in 1677 at a time when commercial documents were in their very infancy—some may regret they have ever grown to adulthood—and when commerce was almost exclusively conducted upon the oral word. In those far away days even the lawyer relied less upon the written document. Court pleadings were often oral. It was Chief Justice Beresford who complained to Counsel at the opening of a case before him: "Get to your business. You plead about one point, they about another, so that neither of you strikes the other."

Much of the original *Statute of Frauds* has been repealed but it still seeks to provide protection against fraud for contracts of guarantee and, as later re-enacted in Section 40 Law of Property Act 1925, for

161

contracts concerning the disposition of land and interests in land. The form of the protection was very simple. The Statute as enacted sought to provide protection against fraud in six classes of contract by requiring that such contracts must be supported by written evidence. Thus a sale of land was not valid unless that sale was recorded in writing. Some 300 years later this simple protection is still available in almost every country whose jurisprudence is based upon the English common law.

Nowadays—and this is what this conference has been convened to consider—it is the written document (whether required or not by law) which itself has become the instrument of fraud. Ironically not only does this simple measure contained in the *Statute of Frauds* not provide protection against fraud but also can actually encourage fraudulent conduct. Let me take an example from the English domestic scene. About nine years ago the descriptive word "gazzump" came into our language. Descriptive it was! When prices were going up day by day sellers of houses were orally agreeing one price with one purchaser one day and on the next day "gazzumping" him by agreeing a new and higher price with another party. Fraudulent conduct it was but actionable under the law it was not. Why? Because an agreement for the sale of land is not binding unless and until it is recorded in writing.

I draw your attention to the *Statute of Frauds*, and its application 300 years later concerning the disposition of interests in land because I believe the law does have responsibility for the extent to which all fraud— not least of which is shipping fraud—is being perpetrated. The plain fact is that in the Baltic Exchange in London, in commodity trading throughout the world and in much other international commerce, there is still enormous reliance upon the oral word and upon consequent and necessary trust between contracting parties. I consider this to be the best protection—bar none—against the perpetration of fraud. It is all part of society setting standards for itself. Indeed it is because fraud was such a serious matter in England that the burden of proof has always been so heavy upon he who alleged fraud. Lord Esher in a case in the House of Lords in 1893 stated "A charge of fraud is such a terrible thing to bring against a man but it cannot be maintained in any Court unless it is shown that he had a wicked mind." However once you move away from the discipline of certain markets and trade associations where it is in the mutual interest of all parties that business is conducted honourably, we must look not only to the vigilance of the trader to make proper enquiries and not to expose himself unnecessarily to the wrong-doings of the rogue but also to the law—domestic and international—to ascertain if the wronged does have proper recourse against the wrong-doer.

In his opening address to the First Seminar on the Prevention of Shipping Fraud, Sir Michael Kerr the distinguished English Advocate and Judge, now Chairman of the Law Commission, stated that the problem of fraud in international shipping, could and should be checked by the practice of disciplines by those engaged in the trade. He recommended a number of simple checks. I am sure that he is right. It is necessary now to spend much more time and effort on prevention of crime. Yet the law itself, in whatever jurisprudence it may rest, should also be given regular attention.

I am not a great enthusiast for International Conventions but perhaps a Code of International Practice should be agreed between the great trading countries of the world. I am awaiting with interest to read the paper which is being produced (with the support of The Baltic and International Maritime Conference) by the International Chamber of Commerce called "Guide to Maritime Fraud Prevention" about which Mr. Sorensen will be later telling us.

I am not sure whether English law would provide the best base for such a code but it would—I hope—make a contribution to the drafting of such a code. Let me therefore sketch out the English law of misrepresentation for you.

B. FRAUD AND MISREPRESENTATION

The pedigree of the modern day law of misrepresentation and fraud is a mixed one. Its origins can be traced back to Statute law and to the Courts of Common Law and Equity. It has also been given recent attention. In the *Misrepresentation Act 1967,* as amended by the *Unfair Contract Terms Act 1977,* Parliament intervened to make some important changes.

Although fraud is often separately described from misrepresentation it is in law a species of misrepresentation. The misrepresentation is fraudulent (and hence a "fraud") when it is made dishonestly and is non-fraudulent (or "innocent") when it is made honestly but inaccurately.

The remedies obtainable from an English Court for misrepresentation are orders for recission and damages. At Common Law the plaintiff is entitled to an Order which permits him to treat the contract as rescinded and enables him to be restored (if possible) to his previous position. Thus if he has paid money or delivered chattels under his contract he is entitled to recover them. However, this Common Law relief does not extend to the award of damages for loss suffered by him on consequence of entering into a contract (or other binding transaction) unless he can further show that the misrepresentation was made fraudulently or (of more recent authority) negligently.

However, before examining further the differing remedies available to parties who take proceedings in England on the grounds of misrepresentation, let us examine the constituents of "misrepresentation" whether it be "fraudulent" or "innocent."

1. *The Form of the Representation*

It must be in some form of a statement but this can be of any variety: it can be oral, written or implied from words or conduct and it can be by way of affirmation, denial, description or otherwise. It has been said that "a nod or a wink, or a shake of the head or a smile" may constitute a representation.

As a general rule, mere silence is not a misrepresentation. There are three general exceptions to this rule:

First, where the contract requires uberrima fides. This is where one party alone to a contract possesses full knowledge of all material facts. In these circumstances he is under a duty to disclose all those material facts to the other party. The outstanding example is a contract for insurance.

Second where a fiduciary relationship exists. This is where there is a relationship of trust, for example between a banker and his client.

Third where the silence itself creates the misrepresentation by misleading the representee into believing a statement of fact which the "silent" representor intentionally wants the representee to believe. A party to a contract may be legally justified in remaining silent about some material fact, but if he makes any statement it must be full and frank. He cannot tell half the facts and thus leave the statement distorted by what has been left unsaid. Also, if a party to a contract makes a statement believing it to be true and subsequently discovers that he was wrong, he must disclose the fact. Similarly, if his statement was true at the time but the facts which it portrays change during the course of negotiations, he is under an obligation to disclose these changes.

2. *The Parties to the Representation*

(a) *The representor*

This is generally the person who makes the representation but can include his principal, his partner and others if they have expressly authorised, tacitly permitted or ratified the representation. Liability will be joint and several and the onus of proof is on the representee.

(b) *The representee*

A representee in law includes (1) any person to whom the representation was directly made, or any principal or partner of such a person; (2) a third party where one person makes a representation to another person, either with an express direction or authority to repeat to a third party, or with intent that it should come to the third party's notice and be acted upon by him; and (3) any member of the public, or of a class, who has acted upon a representation addressed to that public or class. The onus of proof is on the representee.

C. The Nature of a Misrepresentation

A misrepresentation is an untrue statement of fact made by one party (the representor) to another party (the representee) upon which the representor intends the representee to act. The statement must relate to a past or present fact. However, the statement of a *present* intention to do some act in the *future* can amount to a representation if the representee can prove that the intention was non-existent. Thus the Courts (before the imposition of statutory liability under the Companies Acts) readily sided with representees in cases of company prospectuses where for example it was stated that the money would be used in the improvement of buildings and the extension of the business when it was always intended to use the money to discharge existing liabilities.

Although an expression of opinion or a forecast need not be a representation, a statement of finite *expectation* can be (if untrue) actionable as a misrepresentation.

Similarly, where a person who has special knowledge or skill makes representations to another by way of advice, information or opinion, with the intention of inducing the other to enter into a contract with him, the Court of Appeal has held that he is under a duty to use reasonable care to see that the advice, information or opinion is reliable and if he fails in that duty he will be liable for damages for negligence (*Esso Petroleum Company Limited* v. *Mardon* (1976) Q.B. 801).

An action for misrepresentation cannot be founded unless it induced and was intended to induce a representee to make the contract or to otherwise alter his position to his detriment. Thus a misrepresentation will be legally harmless if the representee did not allow it to affect his judgment. While the misrepresentation need not be the sole reason for the representee making the contract, a representee is not entitled to relief if he was aware of the statement's untruth.

D. Types of Misrepresentation

1. *Fraudulent Misrepresentation*

As stated earlier a fraudulent misrepresentation is a false statement which, when made, the representor did not honestly believe to be true. Thus it is the dishonest intent which distinguishes the "fraudulent" from the "innocent" misrepresentation. If a representor honestly believes his statement to be true, he cannot be liable in fraud, no matter how ill advised, stupid, incredulous or negligent he may have been.

2. *Innocent Misrepresentation at Common Law*

It was believed that in English law there could be no liability for damages for financial loss caused by careless words in the absence of a contractual or fiduciary obligation to take care. It has now been established that this view is wrong and that there may exist an independent tortious claim for damages based upon a duty of care if (a) the maker of the statement is possessed of special skill or knowledge or holds himself out as having special skill or knowledge; (b) an undertaking can be implied that he will exercise care in giving informaion and advice; (c) it is foreseeable that the plaintiff will rely on the information and advice and suffer loss if it is inaccurate and (d) it is reasonable for the plaintiff to rely on that information and advice.

3. *Innocent Misrepresentation and the Misrepresentation Act 1967*

The 1967 Act brought the remedies for "innocent" misrepresentation into line with the remedies for fraudulent misrepresentation where a person has entered into a contract after an innocent misrepresentation (*i.e.* non-fraudulent) has been made to him by another party and as a result he has suffered loss, then if the person making the representation would have been liable to damages in respect of it had the misrepresentation been made fraudulently, that person is now liable for damages unless he proves that he had reasonable grounds to believe, and did believe up to the time the contract was made, that the facts represented were true.

E. REMEDIES FOR MISREPRESENTATION

1. *Rescission*

The concept here is to restore the parties to their original positions. Damage has to be proved but the representee must communicate his election to rescind to the representor, which election is treated as final. Rescission is treated as effective from the date it is communicated to the representor but no Order for Rescission can be made where it is impossible to restore parties to their original position or where rescission would deprive a third party of a right in the subject matter of the contract which he has acquired in good faith and for value. In such circumstances the Court has a general power to grant damages in lieu of rescission if it thinks it would be equitable to do so.

Thus Orders for Rescission are rarely made because it is seldom possible to return the parties to their original position. The usual orders are for damages.

2. *Damages.*

The concept is compensation for loss but there is a difference between damages awarded in contract and in tort. In contract the object of damages is to put the injured party as nearly as may be in the position he would have enjoyed if the contract had been performed; in tort it is to restore the injured party to the position he occupied before the tort was committed. This difference means that a greater sum can be obtained in contract than in tort or conversely a greater sum in tort than in contract.

F. DEFENCES TO MISREPRESENTATION

The defences available to the representor follow a pattern of logic. Thus he will have a good defence if he can show that the representee was not misled because he knew the truth. Similarly if he can show that the representee has affirmed the contract and thereby accepted the misrepresentation for what it is. In certain cases, delay can offer a defence. The representor may also be able to claim that by notice or by contractual terms his liability for misrepresentation has been limited or excluded but this term or notice must satisfy the requirement of "reasonableness" introduced in the *Unfair Contract Terms Act 1977*. This is judged by reference to the circumstances which were, or ought reasonably to have been, known to or in the contemplation of the parties when the contract was made and the onus of proof is on the party seeking to rely on the exclusion clause.

G. Concluding Comments

As Judge Haight recognised in his opening comments the role of national laws and courts is limited in protecting society from the perpetration of shipping fraud. The law cannot *prevent* the perpetration of fraud any more than it can make the bad good or the selfish unselfish. The law can set standards for commercial behaviour and courts can enforce those standards. The law can, and in examples which I can give to you from my own country, go further and place requirements upon contracting parties to give notice to the other contracting party of that other party's rights. It has been thought necessary to make such requirements under our Hire Purchase law and under our Landlord and Tenant law where one party can exploit the ignorance or inexperience of the other party. Under our Hire Purchase law the owner of goods under hire purchase has to serve certain notices on the hirer of the goods if the Hire Purchase contract is to be upheld by the courts. Similarly unless a Landlord puts certain information in notices which he gives to his tenant, then that notice is invalid. The effect of such laws is twofold. Firstly, it restrains the exploitation of the less sophisticated party in such transactions. Secondly, it creates a higher awareness to those who should be alert to what they are doing. As has been pointed out by Sir Michael Kerr and speakers at this conference, time and time again fraud is permitted to take place simply because the parties to the transaction were not sufficiently alert or enquiring.

This is precisely the concept behind English law upon contracts uberrima fidei upon which I spoke earlier. Indeed such contracts first received close attention in the field of marine insurance. As long ago as 1822 an English High Court Judge, Mr. Justice Bayley was saying "I think that in all cases of insurance, whether on ships, houses or lives, the underwriter should be informed of every material circumstance within the knowledge of the assured; and that the proper question is, whether any particular circumstance was in fact material, and not whether the party believed it to be so. The contrary doctrine would lead to frequent suppression of information, and it would often be extremely difficult to show that the party neglecting to give the information thought it material. But if it be held that all material facts must be disclosed, it will be in the interest of the assured to make a full and fair disclosure of all the information within their reach."

Thus it was in 1906 that we enacted the Marine Insurance Act which contains, in Section 18(1) this passage:

"Subject to the provisions of this section, the assured must disclose to the insurer, before the contract is concluded, every material circumstance which is known to the assured, and the assured is deemed to know every circumstance which, in the ordinary course of business, ought to be known by him. If the assured fails to make such disclosure, the insurer may avoid the contract."

"Every material circumstance" is defined in Section 18(2) in these terms: 'Every circumstance is material which would influence the judgment of a prudent insurer in fixing the premium, or determining whether he will take the risk.' Under the provisions of our Marine Insurance law, both before the passing of the Act and after it, it has been held that there was a duty on the insured to inform the underwriter that a ship was overdue, or had been put into an immediate port for repair, or that the insured goods were being carried on deck in a place where it was not usual to stack them or that the insured goods were to be taken on board at a port where loading was a hazardous operation.

While the setting of standards, including the requirement for the provision of notices, and the enforcement of those standards through efficient and fair domestic judicial process is of great importance, it does not answer the "international problem" upon how shipping frauds perpetrated on an international scale and not always on the high seas, can be curbed. As Mr. Cooper has just pointed out, there are often a number of countries with a direct interest when a shipping fraud takes place.

As a starter, individual countries could do much to improve the efficacy of extradition treaties. These are, in the main, bilateral agreements but the maritime countries of the world could, in negotiations between one another, ease a lot of the problem. It is certainly sensible that they try to do so. Then consideration should be given to drawing up an international code in which the law concerning fraud and the means by which it can be enforced, could be agreed. It may well be the proposed publication by the international Chamber of Commerce of the "Guide to Maritime Fraud Prevention" will provide a base for the calling of an international conference and the drafting of such an international code.

There is an old saying in England "Where there is a will, there is a way." I am sure this could be so for agreeing measures to combat shipping fraud. It was of early necessity to ship-farers of the world for a Law of the Sea to be agreed and enforced. From time immemorial it has been deemed necessary in the interests of all nations, to treat piracy on the high seas as an international crime against which any nation can take its own action, to detect, apprehend and punish those who indulge in this activity. A pirate, and his ship, lose ipso facto by any act of piracy the protection of their flag state, if they have one, and their national rights. It seems to me that an agreement among nations in which the traditional and limited interpretation of piracy—being an unauthorised act of violence committed by a private vessel on the open sea against another vessel with the intent to plunder—should be widened. It is true, as quoted by Mr. Cooper, that the 1958 Geneva Convention does widen this basic definition but we are still left with the constraint that it is not deemed to be piracy if the acts are performed by the crew against persons or property on the same ship. It is true there could still be a number of shipping frauds which would not be caught in the net of even very broad definition of piracy but it seems to be (and Mr. Paul Sarlis takes up this point in his paper) that agreement between the major commercial countries of the world to permit the apprehension and trial of any national in any ship against whom founded allegations of criminal acts against a ship or its cargo have been made, would be a most effective deterrent. There may be differing views on the quality of one country's trial procedure against another. Possibly an international court could be used but here is a great need for such an initiative to be taken.

Speaking for myself, I much hope that this conference will press forward the much needed public debate on this subject . . . We are in England most concerned over the growth of international shipping fraud and most willing to offer our assistance. In response to international need our Houses of Parliament recently took initiative over international arbitrations. We are most willing to respond again.

INDEX